# Short Stays, Big Pay: The Path to Wealth & Financial Freedom

Build Wealth Fast: Master STRs, Direct Bookings & Platform Strategies for Maximum Profit

Michelle Ward

# Contents


1. Taking the First Step 1
2. Navigating the Wild World of Short-Term Rentals: A No-Nonsense Guide to Avoiding The Pit Falls 4
3. Airbnb: Great Until It Isn't (AKA, Don't Put All Your Bookings in One Basket) 19
4. Beyond Airbnb: Swiping Right on Other Booking Platforms 31
5. Direct Bookings: Cutting Out the Middleman and the Drama 48
6. Setting Up for Success: Branding and Marketing 67
7. The Weird and Wonderful World of Booking.com 87
8. The Underdogs—VRBO, Expedia, and Other Platforms That Deserve a Spot in Your Toolkit 104
9. Building Resilience: Navigating Industry Challenges 125
10. Case Studies and Success Stories – Stories From Some Of The Best 154
11. Future Trends in Short-Term Rentals – What's Next? 170
12. STR Success: Double-Check & Dominate! 185

13. When to Sell, Upgrade, or Expand to Build a Powerful Property Portfolio 191

14. Conclusion 200

About the author 204

References & Suggested Reading 207

# Chapter One

# Taking the First Step

When I started my short-term rental business, I made the classic rookie mistake: I put all my eggs in the Airbnb basket. Don't get me wrong—Airbnb is fantastic. It's user-friendly, has a massive audience, and practically everyone and their dog has heard of it (seriously, some people even list pet-friendly rentals for dogs). But relying solely on one platform? That was a huge oversight. Why? Because as amazing as Airbnb is, it's not the only game in town.

Let's do some quick math. The more platforms your property is listed on, the more eyes see it. The more eyes see it, the more likely it is to get booked. Simple, right? And here's the kicker: in 2024, Booking.com was the most visited travel and tourism website worldwide, with over 500 million online visitors. Yep, you read that right. Half a billion people clicked on Booking.com to plan their travels. They have over 29 million listings spanning more than 220 countries and territories. That's a whole lot of potential guests scrolling through properties—and that's just one platform!

Each property platform has its own unique quirks, criteria, and secret algorithms that determine how and when your listing gets shown. Want to climb the rankings on Booking.com? You'll need to ace things like instant booking, competitive pricing, and stellar reviews. Trying to break into Vrbo's top spots? Better make sure your photos are drool-worthy and your amenities list is packed. And don't even get me started on Plum Guide, the bougiest of them all, where even the coffee maker you choose could make or break your application.

Then there are the regional platforms, like Stayz in Australia or Holidu in Europe, that cater to niche markets. These platforms might not have the same global reach as the giants, but they come with their own loyal customer base—and often less competition. Listing on these smaller platforms can sometimes mean fewer headaches, as their support teams tend to be more hands-on and personal.

But wait, there's more! While these platforms are great for exposure, they all come with their own fees. And those fees? Well, they can add up faster than a guest accidentally breaking your favorite vase. This is where direct bookings come into play. Direct bookings are the ultimate game-changer. When you get a guest to book directly with you, you're cutting out the middleman. No fees, no commissions, just sweet, sweet profit straight into your pocket.

Direct bookings also give you more control. Want to offer a special discount for returning guests? Done. Need to update your house rules without waiting for platform approval? Easy. Plus, building a direct booking strategy allows you to create a personal brand for your properties, giving guests a reason to choose you over the sea of faceless listings.

That's why I wrote this book. I want to take you beyond Airbnb and show you how to make the most out of every booking platform while also building a strategy to secure those coveted direct bookings. Whether you're a seasoned host or just starting out, my goal is to help you get maximum exposure for your properties and, more importantly, make as much money as possible ( isn't that the point?).

So, buckle up! In this chapter, we'll start by exploring the major platforms, their strengths and weaknesses, and how to leverage them to your advantage. We'll also dip our toes into the world of direct bookings and why they're the holy grail of hosting. Later, we'll dive into practical tips like creating a killer website, setting up payment systems, and building a loyal guest base. It's time to take your short-term rental business to the next level.

## Chapter Two

# Navigating the Wild World of Short-Term Rentals: A No-Nonsense Guide to Avoiding The Pit Falls

So, you've decided to dive into the short-term rental world—congrats! Before you roll out the welcome mat, get comfy because it's time to explore the many platforms where you can showcase your home sweet rental. This chapter is your friendly guide to understanding the differences between major and alternative platforms, what fees might nibble at your profits, and which features can help your property stand out in the sea of listings. Let's break it all down, with a dash of humor and a warm embrace of practicality.

## Differentiate Between Major and Alternative Platforms

Think of this as choosing between a big-box store and a charming boutique. Sure, the big-box store has the recognition, the shiny ads, and a return policy so lenient it makes you question humanity. But the boutique? Oh, the boutique has character. It's where you find that one-of-a-kind piece you can't stop bragging about. In this section, we'll weigh the pros and cons of major players like Airbnb—the Target of short-term rentals—and those hidden gems of platforms that might just become your secret weapon. Think of them as the quirky, offbeat shops where magic happens. One platform might bring you steady, predictable bookings; the other might bring you the kind of guests who book for two weeks and leave behind a bottle of wine as a thank-you. The goal?

Finding the perfect balance between scale and charm, so your rental feels like a curated experience instead of an aisle in a rental superstore. Let's figure out which platforms deserve a spot in your retail... uh, rental strategy!

## Definition of Major Platforms

Major platforms like Airbnb are the Goliaths of the rental world, stomping around with their massive market share, global audience reach, and name recognition that even your grandma knows (and she still calls it "Air B&B&B"). They're the go-to choice for everyone, from your tech-savvy niece who books vacations based on Instagrammable views, to your retired neighbor who's still trying to figure out how to attach a selfie to their profile. These platforms are the rental equivalent of the biggest party in town—everyone's there, and they all brought a plus-one.

**Lesson** Visibility is fantastic, but with great market share comes fierce competition. It's not enough to just show up; you need to dazzle. Hosts need to master the art of standing out in a crowd, which means turning your listing into the peacock in a field of pigeons—bright, bold, and basically saying, "Look at me!" But let's be clear: this isn't about slapping a neon "Hot Deal!" banner on your listing. It's about nailing those tiny details that make guests scroll, click, and say, "This is it!" Think stellar photos, killer descriptions, and amenities that whisper (or shout), "Pick me, I'm awesome!" Remember, when you're up against a million listings offering "cozy stays" and "charming decor," you need to give guests a reason to stop mid-scroll and say, "Forget the rest—I want the peacock."

## Definition of Alternative Platforms

Alternative platforms are the hidden gems of the hosting world—the cool indie cafes compared to Starbucks. They cater to niche audiences who know exactly what they want, whether it's eco-friendly travelers who refuse single-use plastics or luxury seekers who think a regular bathtub is an insult to their vacation aspirations. These platforms might not have the massive market share of Airbnb or Vrbo, but what they lack in size, they make up for in personality—and fewer hosts competing for attention. It's like finding a quiet corner of the internet where your rental can be the star of the show instead of just another listing lost in the noise.

**Lesson:** These platforms often come with quirky fee structures, unique requirements, or that one rule that makes you go, "Wait, what?" But don't let that scare you off. They offer a chance to shine in front of the right audience without fighting the masses. It's like discovering a farmers' market after years of shopping at the same crowded supermarket. Sure, you'll pay more for the artisanal cheese, but you're also getting something way better than a shrink-wrapped block of cheddar. Diversifying into alternative platforms is like sprinkling paprika into your rental strategy—it's unexpected, it's bold, and it'll make people wonder what you're cooking. Whether you're aiming to attract guests who want an off-grid yurt with compost toilets or those who won't book unless the thread count hits quadruple digits, these platforms give you room to shine like the rental rockstar you are. Bonus: you'll also rack up serious bragging rights when you casually drop, "Oh, I'm on this exclusive site for sustainable stays," into conversation.

## Comparison of User Experiences

Ever notice how some websites feel like a cozy blanket fresh out of the dryer, while others make you feel like you just signed up for a calculus exam on a Friday afternoon? It's wild how the design of a platform can totally change the vibe of your guest experience. I mean, if your guests are greeted by a website that looks like it was made in the early 2000s—complete with pixelated images and a thousand pop-ups—don't be surprised if they start questioning their life choices. On the flip side, a sleek, intuitive site that flows like the perfect cup of coffee? Now that might just convince someone to book. Your platform's user interface is essentially your first impression. It's like the welcoming handshake before you've even said "hello." If it's easy to navigate, feels smooth, and is a treat to look at, people will actually stick around to see what you've got to offer. It's like dating apps: if the photos are blurry, or if you have to do 10 clicks just to see a picture of the property, you're probably not going to score a date—or in this case, a booking. But when your platform matches your brand and your guests' expectations, it's like hitting a home run in a baseball game where the crowd goes wild.

**Lesson:** Choose a platform that vibes with both your brand and your target guest like a perfect pair of socks. It's all about that strategic positioning! When you nail this, your guest retention can soar like a kite in the wind—and best of all, you'll avoid the headaches of juggling endless questions about how to click through the booking page. Keep it smooth, keep it stylish, and keep it simple!

## Market Positioning

Imagine this: the major booking platforms are like the giant concert stages—bright lights, booming speakers, and thousands of people screaming for a glimpse of what's on offer. It's a wild ride, but you're just one act in a long line-up, hoping your performance stands out in the crowd. The alternative platforms, on the other hand, are like cozy little cafes—dim lighting, the smell of fresh espresso in the air, and a laid-back crowd who came for the vibe, not the crowd. Your offering needs to match the mood of whichever "venue" you choose—because let's face it, you wouldn't wear a tux to a casual coffee shop, right? When you're picking a platform, it's like choosing between a rock concert and an intimate acoustic set. If you're trying to rock out on a tiny stage with your massive property, well, things might get awkward. And if you show up to a festival with your quaint little cabin in the woods expecting an arena crowd... it's probably going to feel a bit out of place. Understand your audience—are they looking for a luxurious, all-inclusive experience on the big stage, or do they want a unique, personal experience that feels like a home away from home in that little café? Once you've got that figured out, tailor your unique selling proposition to match the platform's audience. For example, your "rustic charm" might be a hit on a more niche, boutique site, while the same cabin might get lost in the shuffle on a major platform where people are booking high-end villas and city apartments.

**Lesson:** You can't please everyone, and let's be honest, trying to would probably give you a headache. But you can absolutely wow your ideal guest if you find the right place to showcase your space and cater to what they're looking for. So pick your venue wisely, rock it like you own the place, and let the bookings roll in! Just remember, whether you're performing at a packed stadium or a hidden gem of a café, make sure you're playing the right tunes for the right crowd. By understanding the distinctions between platforms, you'll gain a strategic edge. It's like choosing the right fishing spot—cast your net wisely and reel in the perfect catch.

## Analyze Fees and Charges on Each Platform

Nobody likes surprise fees. It's like ordering a burger, and when it arrives, the ketchup is somehow extra. When it comes to booking platforms, you want to know exactly who's taking a slice of your hard-earned pie, and how much of it. Because trust me, understanding fee structures is like knowing who's bringing what dish to the party—you don't want to show up with a casserole only to find out someone's already serving lasagna, and you're stuck with the bill for the entire spread.

Platforms are like houseguests. Some are the polite types who show up, bring a bottle of wine, and even help with the dishes. They'll take a fair commission and be on their way. Then, there are the others—those freeloaders who raid your fridge like it's an all-you-can-eat buffet, leave crumbs everywhere, and somehow manage to rack up the electricity so high that you'd think they were booking a VIP suite instead of a cozy cabin.

You've got your commissions, service fees, cleaning charges, and all sorts of other sneaky little costs lurking in the background like a ninja. It's like playing Monopoly and realizing the "community chest" card you drew is actually a tax audit. Platforms could take anywhere from 3% to 20% or more of your booking, and understanding where those cuts are coming from is key to avoiding any financial surprises that leave you feeling like you've been hit with a hidden surcharge just for breathing.

**Lesson:** Get a solid understanding of the fee structures before you even think about pricing your property. Know who's taking what and make sure you're not left paying the price for someone else's high-maintenance behavior. With this knowledge in your back pocket, you'll price your property smartly and avoid having to explain to your guests why that "charming" two-bedroom cabin now costs the same as a luxury penthouse. Plus, when you're upfront about pricing and fees, you'll build trust with your guests—and trust means repeat bookings, fewer complaints, and a much happier you. In the end, the clearer you are about the fees, the fewer "surprises" you'll have on your balance sheet. And honestly, who needs more surprises? We've all got enough of those in life (like when your friend shows up to dinner with a "plus one" you weren't expecting). Keep it simple, keep it transparent, and watch your guests appreciate the honesty—and your wallet appreciate the lack of hidden charges.

## Strategies for Reducing Fees

Ah, direct bookings—my all-time favorite! It's like cutting out the middleman at a dinner party and going straight to the host for the best seat at the table. No awkward pleasantries, no waiting in line, just you and your guest enjoying the experience—minus those pesky commission fees. Booking platforms are like that overly enthusiastic friend who insists on taking a cut of everything, even the smallest victories. They love the spotlight, but let's be honest: We should be the ones soaking up all the glory, right? Less commission, more profit, and you get to keep all the credit. It's the dream, really. Now, you might be wondering, why on earth do booking platforms take 15% or more of your hard-earned cash? Well, think of it like this: they're throwing the big party. They've got the stage, the confetti, the giant banners, and even a few dance floors—but you're the one who's supplying the snacks, music, and drinks (aka your lovely property). So, they throw in a little "cover charge," or rather, a big ol' slice of your pie, for all that exposure. They argue it's worth it to get your listing in front of the masses, but let's be honest—sometimes it feels like you're paying them to be in a crowd of other property listings, all while they're enjoying the lion's share of the attention and income. The good news? Direct bookings are your golden ticket. By building relationships with your guests and taking matters into your own hands, you get to keep all that sweet, sweet revenue for yourself. You get to skip the middleman entirely (sorry, not sorry, booking platforms), and guess what? Guests love feeling special. It's like when you get an invitation to a private VIP event—you know, the kind where you don't have to elbow your way through a crowd of a thousand people just to get a glimpse of the host. They feel important, and you get to personally roll out the red carpet. What's not to love?

You have to play by the rules. No platform likes to feel like it's being hustled, so encourage direct bookings without breaking any platform rules. It's like flirting with the idea of skipping the group project but still being polite enough to turn in your assignment on time (aka, keep the platform happy). But once you've got those direct bookings rolling in, you can watch your profits soar like a rocket into the atmosphere, and your wallet will be doing a happy dance—while booking platforms are left staring from the sidelines.

**Lesson:** Understanding those platform fees and how they can eat away at your profits is step one. But with some clever strategies in place, you can bypass the middleman, keep your pricing competitive, and watch your business thrive without sharing the wealth. You get to keep the spotlight on you, and everyone loves a little extra cash in their pocket.

## Assess Unique Features and Offerings of Platforms

What makes a platform sparkle? Think of your rental listing as a first date—it needs to stand out, charm the socks off your guests, and leave them dreaming of a second visit. This section dives into the bells, whistles, and glitter cannons that can turn your rental into the prom queen of the platform. From jaw-dropping photography to irresistible perks, let's roll out the red carpet for your future guests (and their wallets).

## Platform Unique Selling Propositions

Some platforms are like a matchmaking service for specific types of guests. You've got the ones that roll out the welcome mat for pet lovers, the ones that cater exclusively to digital nomads with a passion for remote work, and then there are those that are more like the "nightclub" for luxury seekers. These platforms each have their own flavor, and understanding them can seriously shape your strategy. It's like finding the right pair of shoes—you don't want to wear flip-flops to a black-tie event, right? Take, for example, pet-friendly platforms. These are the places where people are looking for a place that will accept their beloved furry companions (who, let's be honest, probably have more Instagram followers than you). If your place is decked out with dog beds, toys, and a fenced-in yard perfect for playtime, you'll thrive on a platform like that. But here's the kicker—don't list your pet-friendly space on a platform that's a haven for cat lovers if you're more of a "dog only" kind of host. You're setting yourself up for a passive-aggressive cat-lover rebellion. They'll be making passive-aggressive comments like, "Oh, I love dogs... when they're not chewing on my favorite shoes." Not the kind of vibes we're going for. Then, there are the platforms designed for digital nomads. They want fast Wi-Fi, ergonomic chairs, and maybe a free coffee machine to fuel their hustle. They're not just looking for a cute place to stay—they need an office, a sanctuary, and probably a weekly yoga session to balance their "work-life" (which might actually just be "work-until-you-pass-out" life). If your rental has a cozy desk, a stellar internet connection, and a coffee shop vibe, this is your crowd. But if your place is more of a "beachfront bliss" experience with no Wi-Fi in sight, you're going to have some unhappy nomads checking in, only to check out two hours later because their Zoom call couldn't load.

**Lesson:** Know your audience—understand which platform's vibe matches your property and tailor your offerings accordingly. Align your space with the right crowd, whether they're traveling with their four-legged friends, working from a hammock, or just seeking the perfect weekend getaway. Cat lovers need not apply if your place is dog-friendly (or vice versa). And digital nomads don't want to end up in a place where they can't even upload their latest "working from the beach" photo. Tailoring your listing to the right platform ensures you don't get caught in the crossfire of mismatched expectations. Everyone wins, you get the right guests, and no one has to negotiate over who gets to sleep on the couch.

## Marketing Support

Ah, promotional tools—every platform's attempt to "help" you boost your visibility and get those bookings rolling in. It's like a neon sign flashing "Look at me!" except it's also asking you to give up a slice of your pie for the privilege. Some platforms offer perks like discounts for first-time guests or featured listings to get you some extra eyeballs. But here's the catch: while it might seem like a good idea to get some quick bookings and reviews, these discounts don't just disappear into thin air—they come out of your bottom line.

Take Airbnb's first-booking promotion, for example. They offer a 20% discount on your first three bookings to get you some reviews and fast-track your popularity. Sounds great, right? Who doesn't want those shiny, sparkling reviews to boost their credibility? The problem is, you don't get to pick when the guests arrive. So, imagine this: you've got a cozy little cabin that's perfect for a summer getaway, and suddenly, during peak season, someone books at a 20% discount. What happens? You end up giving away a chunk of your earnings right when you could've charged top dollar. It's like agreeing to a Black Friday deal and then realizing you've got a line of people ready to snatch up your products at 20% off, just when you were hoping for a full-price sale. Ouch. I can tell you from personal experience, it stings. It's like you've been hyped up for a big win, and then bam—20% of your hard-earned cash goes straight out the window during a peak period. The goal might be to help you get those reviews quickly, but you can't always predict the timing, and that's a gamble.

**Lesson:** Leverage these promotional tools to boost visibility, especially during the low season when you're trying to fill up those slow months. Use those discounts to grab some attention when business is quieter, not when everyone and their grandma is booking last-minute getaways at full price. No matter how many times Booking.com or Airbnb tells you to "opt in for extra visibility," there's no reason to throw your money away during peak season when you could be charging full rates and raking in the cash. It's like putting a sale sticker on your best-selling items when everyone's shopping for them—don't do it. Save those promotional tools for the off-season when things are a little slower, and your guests will appreciate the deal while you still get to keep more of the money in your pocket. Trust me, your wallet will thank you, and you won't be left feeling like you've given away the store during the busiest time of the year. Keep that discount in your back pocket until the crowd clears—there's no shame in playing the long game.

## Final thoughts

Navigating the short-term rental landscape can sometimes feel like trying to read a treasure map while standing on a moving pirate ship—it's a little chaotic, a little confusing, and honestly, you might spill some rum along the way. But here's the secret: think of it like a treasure hunt. Every platform is like a different spot on that map, each with its own set of opportunities (and hidden dangers, of course). With the right strategy and a little bit of savvy, you'll find the gold—or at least a chest full of shiny reviews and steady bookings.

Each platform comes with its own quirks, kind of like how every treasure hunter has their own unique skill set. Some platforms are all about the flash and glamour, drawing in guests with fancy marketing and massive reach. Others are like the hidden gems—those cozy, niche spots that cater to specific audiences, like pet lovers or digital nomads. Think of it like choosing between a crowded tourist trap or a secret beach where only the coolest people hang out. Sure, the tourist trap is packed with people, but do you really want to fight for space on a towel? Probably not. Find your secret beach (or your perfect platform), and own it.

Take the time to explore and experiment with these platforms. It's like dating—sometimes you need to date around a bit before you find the perfect match. Don't be afraid to try out different strategies, see what works, and then double down on what gets you the best results. Embrace the quirks of each platform, because let's be real, if everything was perfect and easy, it'd be way too boring. A little bit of unpredictability keeps things interesting, and who doesn't love a good plot twist?

Your rental success story starts right here—today, this very moment, while you're reading this and mentally preparing to tackle that next big decision. It's like setting sail on an adventure—sure, you might encounter some storms (those pesky platform fees, guest complaints, or unexpected cancellations), but with your eyes on the prize, you'll weather them just fine. So, grab that treasure map, keep your compass pointed toward those direct bookings, and remember: the gold is out there.

I've **tripped, stumbled, and faceplanted** my way through short-term rental hosting so you don't have to. Consider this checklist your **friendly (and slightly sarcastic) reminder** to avoid the classic STR rookie mistakes. I've **burned through budgets, under priced stays, trusted guests a little too much (looking at you, Mr. "I Swear My Dog Doesn't Shed"),** and learned these lessons the hard way. But lucky for you, I took the hits so you can **glide into hosting success with ease**. So, whenever you're feeling unsure, overwhelmed, or just need a quick reality check—**flip to this list at the end of the book!** It's like a cheat sheet for STR domination, minus the stress. And hey, if you **do** end up making a few mistakes along the way, don't sweat it—just make sure they're the kind that lead to **funny stories, not financial disasters.**

Chapter Three

# Airbnb: Great Until It Isn't (AKA, Don't Put All Your Bookings in One Basket)

Airbnb, the giant of the short-term rental world. It's like the popular kid in school: always getting the attention, always at the top of the rankings, and always the first one to be invited to the party. And for good reason! Airbnb brought the world of short-term rentals into the mainstream and made hosting accessible to millions. You get the perks of massive visibility, a user-friendly platform, and a sense of community that makes you feel like you're part of a bigger movement. For hosts, it's like being handed the keys to a bustling metropolis, with potential guests knocking at your door from every corner of the globe.

But here's the thing: even the most popular kid in school has a few quirks. And as dominant as Airbnb is, it comes with its own set of limitations that can leave even the most seasoned hosts scratching their heads. From hefty service fees that can eat into your profits, to unpredictable algorithm changes that leave your listing feeling like a forgotten back row seat at the prom—Airbnb isn't all sunshine and rainbows. For every benefit of exposure and guest trust, there's a downside that can make you feel like you're losing out more than you're gaining.

So, what's the lesson here? It's about balancing those benefits and constraints—leveraging Airbnb's massive reach to fill your calendar while being mindful of the platform's fees and rules. Understanding both sides of the coin lets you make smarter decisions, so you can still enjoy the spotlight without getting bogged down by the platform's occasional frustrations.

In the end, Airbnb offers a unique opportunity, but it's important to know its limits and use that knowledge to your advantage. Because let's face it, we all love a little extra income, but we also deserve a little peace of mind. By navigating the benefits and constraints of Airbnb with a clear strategy, you'll be able to ride the wave of success without getting swept under by the occasional storm.

## Impact of Airbnb's Policies on Hosts

Airbnb's constantly evolving policies can significantly impact the operational freedom and profitability of hosts, leading to a fair amount of confusion and frustration. Over the years, the platform has introduced a variety of policy changes—ranging from adjustments to cleaning fees, cancellation policies, guest verification processes, to the introduction of new booking requirements—that can create a sense of unpredictability for hosts trying to manage their business effectively. For instance, the introduction of standardized cleaning fees or a cap on service charges might seem like an effort to streamline the process, but it can also limit hosts' ability to set prices based on their individual needs or the specifics of their property.

These sudden policy shifts not only make it more difficult for hosts to accurately forecast their earnings, but they also reduce the flexibility that hosts once enjoyed in managing their listings. Without warning, new restrictions can be imposed on how and when bookings are accepted, or changes to the platform's algorithm can push a host's listing further down in search rankings, limiting exposure. In addition, these changes can also impact the level of guest interaction—some policies might even make it harder for hosts to connect personally with guests or screen them effectively. For example, Airbnb's introduction of stricter guest vetting procedures or mandatory instant booking can reduce a host's ability to make personalized decisions about who stays in their home. This, in turn, can decrease the overall guest experience and lower the potential for repeat business. Hosts may also find themselves juggling last-minute booking rules, automatic cancellation policies, or guest complaints that they have little control over.

To maintain profitability and avoid penalties, hosts must stay informed and adapt quickly to these ever-changing regulations. Failure to do so can lead to significant losses, especially when it comes to booking cancellations, handling disputes, or dealing with the consequences of not adhering to the latest rules. In the end, navigating Airbnb's fluctuating policies requires hosts to be not only flexible and adaptable but also diligent in staying updated on any policy shifts that may impact their operations. This added complexity can make running an Airbnb business feel more like a constant game of catch-up, where hosts are required to keep one step ahead just to stay afloat.

## Support Systems

Airbnb's support systems can often feel like a maze—you know, the kind where you're trying to find the exit but every turn leads to another dead end. While the platform's support team is, of course, there to help, the reality is that their services can be inconsistent and, at times, downright frustrating. Hosts often find themselves trying to navigate a maze of help articles that are written in what feels like a foreign language, or waiting on hold for an eternity to get someone on the phone—who may or may not be able to help. This lack of timely support can create major challenges, especially when issues arise during peak booking periods when you don't have time to twiddle your thumbs while waiting for a resolution.

The situation gets even trickier when Airbnb's guidelines are complicated and somewhat ambiguous, leaving hosts to feel like they need a PhD in customer service just to understand what's required. Hosts may spend hours combing through FAQs or scrolling through endless threads in community forums, only to find that the answer they need is still elusive. It's like trying to solve a Rubik's Cube blindfolded—just when you think you've got it figured out, you end up right back where you started. And let's not even get started on the "help" chatbots that send you in circles, only to finally offer a response like, "We're experiencing high volume, please try again later." Classic.

The lack of clarity in Airbnb's support structure can lead to a sense of discouragement, making hosts feel like they're navigating this complex business on their own, without the backup they need to keep things running smoothly. But here's the thing: a well-structured, clear, and accessible support system can completely change the game. When hosts can quickly access helpful advice, get a direct response from someone who actually knows what they're talking about, and feel like their concerns are taken seriously, it can make all the difference. It reduces stress, boosts confidence, and keeps hosts motivated to manage their listings proactively.

Ultimately, Airbnb's support system could use a little TLC to make it more reliable, accessible, and user-friendly. If hosts could spend more time hosting and less time troubleshooting, they'd be able to provide better experiences for their guests—and have more fun doing it. It is better for Superhosts but still very frustrating at times. Imagine a world where support is as quick as a message and as clear as a sunny day. That world would be a lot less stressful, and maybe, just maybe, Airbnb would be the truly supportive partner we all wish it could be.

That said, if you think Airbnb is challenging, buckle up, because Booking.com is like the rollercoaster you didn't sign up for, and you're not even sure if the seatbelt works. Seriously, get ready for a whole new level of frustration that'll make you look back at Airbnb and say, "You know what? You're not that bad." But hold that thought—more on the wild ride that is Booking.com later. I'll just say this: it's like hosting with a backpack full of bricks, and half of them are on fire. Stay tuned.

## Market Share and Reach of Airbnb

To take a closer look at Airbnb's reign as the king of short-term rentals—and let's face it, it's wearing the crown with all the confidence of a pageant queen—we need to evaluate what its dominance really means for us, the humble hosts. On the one hand, Airbnb has revolutionized the market, turning spare rooms and vacation homes into thriving businesses. It's like they handed us the keys to the kingdom, complete with millions of potential guests browsing for their perfect getaway. On the other hand, their dominance comes with a few strings attached—some are subtle, and others feel more like trying to untangle holiday lights in a rush.

For one, their influence is so massive that hosts almost feel required to play by their rules or risk missing out on a flood of potential bookings. And while they've created a platform with incredible visibility, the implications for hosts aren't always as sparkly as the marketing makes it sound. From fluctuating algorithms to ever-changing policies and fees, Airbnb can feel less like a dependable partner and more like that friend who borrows your stuff and gives it back with "just a few changes."

Their grip on the market also means they have the power to dictate trends, which can force hosts to adapt, even when the changes don't necessarily align with their business goals. Whether it's mandatory discounts, unclear support systems, or policies that make you question if you're still in charge of your own property, hosting on Airbnb can be both a blessing and a test of patience.

So, what's the verdict on their dominance? It's a double-edged sword. On the bright side, they've opened doors (literally), connected hosts to guests from all over the world, and made short-term rentals a viable and even lucrative option for many. On the flip side, their market power means hosts often have to make peace with the less-than-perfect aspects of the platform. But hey, no kingdom is without its flaws, and as hosts, we've learned to adapt, innovate, and thrive—even when the Airbnb empire throws us a curveball. Stay tuned, because this is just the tip of the iceberg—there's a lot more to unpack when it comes to the implications of Airbnb's rule over the short-term rental market.

**Lesson:** As a host, understanding Airbnb's market dynamics isn't just a nice-to-have—it's a survival skill. Think of it as learning to ride a unicycle while juggling flaming torches. Sure, it looks glamorous, but one wrong move, and you're left trying to figure out how to extinguish a fire and save your balance. To thrive on this platform, you've got to master the art of leveraging its benefits while sidestepping its many little traps and quirks.

Airbnb gives you visibility, guests, and a global stage to showcase your property—it's like getting handed a shiny, golden ticket to the short-term rental big leagues. But the catch? That ticket comes with fine print, and if you don't read it closely, you might end up wondering why your wallet feels a little lighter or why your once-cozy listing now feels like a full-time job.

It's all about finding the sweet spot. Use Airbnb's massive reach to your advantage—woo those guests, collect those reviews, and bask in the glow of five-star ratings. But don't be afraid to call out the downsides, either. Stay on top of policy changes, keep an eye on those sneaky fees, and remember: just because Airbnb suggests something (like offering a 20% discount during peak season) doesn't mean you have to follow blindly.

## Challenges Faced by Hosts Relying Solely on Airbnb

It's easy to fall into the rhythm of depending on the platform that makes everything seem so simple: guests come to you, payments are processed, and voilà—success, right? Not so fast. Relying solely on Airbnb is like leaning too far back in your chair—sure, it works for a while, but the moment something shifts, you're on the floor wondering what went wrong. Here's why depending on just one platform is riskier than leaving a toddler alone with a chocolate cake.

## Dependency Risks: Airbnb as Your Single Point of Failure

When you put all your energy into Airbnb and Airbnb alone, you're building your empire on rented land. Yes, Airbnb's reach is massive, and the bookings might flow in like a river during rainy season—but what happens when the rain stops? Market fluctuations, algorithm changes, or global events (hello, pandemic) can turn that river into a trickle faster than you can say "booking request." If Airbnb decides to favor newer hosts or shift its policies, your well-oiled rental business could suddenly feel more like a rusty bicycle.

Let's not forget those horror stories of hosts waking up to find their accounts suspended without warning or explanation. One moment, you're riding high, and the next, you're frantically Googling "how to recover deleted Airbnb listings." Without a backup plan, this could spell disaster for your income stream. Diversification—using multiple platforms and encouraging direct bookings—is like installing a safety net. It keeps you afloat even if Airbnb decides you're yesterday's news.

## Loss of Control: Whose Property Is It Anyway?

As a host, you'd think you'd be in charge, right? Wrong. Relying solely on Airbnb often means playing by their rules, whether you like it or not. Platform-mandated changes are a regular occurrence, from forced discounts to mandatory cancellation policies, and they're about as welcome as a raccoon at a picnic. These changes can derail your carefully crafted management style, leaving you to adapt to decisions you had no say in.

Then there's the guest contact limitation. Sure, Airbnb lets you message your guests, but only through their platform and with a strict set of rules. Want to send your guest a friendly tip about local attractions? Better make sure it doesn't sound like you're encouraging them to book directly next time—or the algorithm police might come knocking. This lack of autonomy can feel stifling, especially when you know that building genuine relationships is the key to guest loyalty and glowing reviews.

The solution? Diversify your approach with tools and strategies that let you engage with guests outside of Airbnb's walled garden.

## Fees and Commissions: The Silent Profit Killer

Let's talk money. Airbnb's service fees might seem small at first, but over time, they add up—like that one friend who keeps "borrowing" your fries. Between guest service fees and host commissions, a good chunk of your earnings disappears before it even hits your bank account. And don't forget those promotional discounts that Airbnb loves to suggest (read: insist). Sure, they claim it's to boost your visibility, but when you're giving away 20% during peak season, it feels less like a boost and more like a sucker punch to your profits.

Understanding these fee structures is essential to staying profitable. Hosts who take the time to analyze how much they're actually earning after fees can adjust their pricing strategies accordingly—or better yet, explore platforms with more favorable terms. Trust me, there's a whole world beyond Airbnb, and some of it comes with lower fees and fewer headaches.

## Brand Identity: Standing Out in the Airbnb Sea of Sameness

Airbnb is a massive marketplace where everything from cozy treehouses to futuristic shipping containers competes for attention. While the variety is amazing for guests, for hosts, it's a bit like showing up to a talent show where everyone's juggling flaming swords—you need something truly spectacular to stand out. Without a distinct brand identity, your listing can get lost faster than a sock in the laundry.

Establishing a unique brand is your ticket to rising above the crowd and catching the eye of your ideal guests. Think of it this way: if your rental is just another "modern apartment with a great view," you're practically blending into Airbnb's wallpaper. But, if you're "the quirky avocado-themed condo where every guest gets guacamole on arrival," suddenly you've got something memorable—and who doesn't love guac?

Successful branding isn't just about flashy gimmicks (although they help). It's about crafting an experience that makes guests want to hit that "Book Now" button without a second thought. Maybe it's a playful theme, exceptional amenities, or simply the fact that your listing description reads like a heartfelt love letter to potential guests rather than a generic sales pitch. Whatever it is, creative marketing is your best friend. Lean into storytelling, highlight your unique features, and make your property irresistible.

Social media can be a game-changer here, too. A well-curated Instagram page or a viral TikTok showcasing your rental's charm can draw in guests before they even make it to Airbnb. Bonus points if you can turn your past guests into ambassadors by encouraging reviews and user-generated content. Word of mouth still works wonders, even if it's digital.

In the vast Airbnb marketplace, standing out requires effort, creativity, and a touch of boldness. But when you nail it, your brand becomes more than just a listing—it becomes an experience guests can't stop raving about. And when guests remember you as "that incredible place with the quirky decor and free guacamole," you know you're doing something right.

## The Takeaway: Diversify, Take Control, and Keep More of Your Pie

Relying solely on Airbnb is like showing up to a potluck with just one dish—if it flops, you're going hungry. And let's be real, nobody wants to be the person stuck eating dry casserole while everyone else is feasting on a full spread. That's why diversifying your booking channels isn't just a good idea—it's survival.

By branching out to multiple platforms, building direct booking strategies, and exploring creative alternatives, you're not just avoiding disaster; you're setting yourself up for long-term success. Think of it like spreading your eggs across several baskets—and maybe keeping a few in your own fridge for good measure (because let's face it, sometimes you just want breakfast on your own terms).

Platforms come and go, algorithms change on a whim, and fees have a way of creeping up faster than your favorite coffee shop's prices. But when you take control of your business—your listings, your guests, your marketing—you're no longer at the mercy of someone else's rulebook. You get to call the shots, keep more of your hard-earned money, and provide an even better experience for your guests.

So don't put all your trust (or bookings) in one place. Get creative, stay flexible, and remember: the sky's the limit—no platform can hold you back. And if one ever tries? Well, you've got a whole buffet of options waiting.

Chapter Four

# Beyond Airbnb: Swiping Right on Other Booking Platforms

When it comes to branching out beyond Airbnb, platforms like Vrbo, B ooking.com, and Expedia are ready to mingle—each with its own quirks, benefits, and, let's be honest, occasional headaches. Vrbo (short for Vacation Rentals by Owner) is the go-to for family-friendly stays and larger properties. It's perfect if your rental screams, "Bring the kids, grandparents, and even the dog!" Guests here tend to book for longer stays, which means fewer turnovers for you—winning!

Then there's Booking.com, the platform that feels like the overachiever of the group. It offers massive exposure and caters to everyone from business travelers to vacationers, but be warned: their interface is about as user-friendly as a manual for assembling IKEA furniture blindfolded and the host support is terrible. Finally, Expedia operates like a travel superstore, bundling your property with flights, car rentals, and activities. It's ideal for guests planning big trips, but as a host, you might feel like just one item on the shelf.

Exploring these platforms is like speed-dating for your property—each offers unique perks, but none are perfect. With a little experimentation, though, you might just find the right fit that brings in bookings while keeping you (mostly) sane.

## Features and Advantages of Vrbo: Why It's the Cool Aunt of Booking Platforms

If Airbnb is the prom queen of short-term rentals, Vrbo is like the cool aunt who shows up with snacks, tells hilarious stories, and lets you stay up past your bedtime. With its unique features and advantages, Vrbo can be a game-changer for hosts looking to diversify and connect with a different kind of guest. Let's break down what makes this platform shine—and why it's worth considering as part of your rental strategy.

## Target Market Focus: Big Groups, Bigger Opportunities

Vrbo knows its audience, and spoiler alert: it's not the solo traveller just looking for a weekend getaway. This platform is all about families and groups. Whether it's a multi-generational family vacation, a reunion of college friends, or a bunch of parents escaping their kids for a "business retreat," Vrbo is the place they go to find properties that fit their needs.

The focus on entire home rentals is a huge win for hosts with spacious properties. Guests aren't searching for "private rooms" or "cozy shared spaces"—they want the whole place, preferably with enough bedrooms and bathrooms to keep Uncle Bob's snoring from waking everyone up. By emphasizing family-friendly features like cribs, game rooms, or pools, you can make your listing irresistible to this demographic. Who doesn't want to be the host of choice for Aunt Karen's epic family reunion?

## User-Friendly Interface: Easy on the Eyes, Easy on the Brain

If you've ever wrestled with a clunky platform that feels like solving a Rubik's cube blindfolded (looking at you, Booking.com), Vrbo will feel like a breath of fresh air. Its intuitive design is a lifesaver for both guests and hosts. For guests, the search filters are straightforward, making it easy for them to find exactly what they need—whether that's "oceanfront villa" or "cozy cabin with Wi-Fi so Dad can pretend he's working."

For hosts, managing listings is almost...fun? The platform is designed to save time, with tools that streamline updates and inquiries. Plus, the enhanced visibility features ensure your property gets seen by the right people. It's like having a spotlight on your rental, minus the nerve-wracking pressure of a talent show. And higher conversion rates? That's just the cherry on top.

## Longer Stays: Less Hustle, More Revenue

If the rapid turnover of Airbnb bookings has you feeling like you're running a full-time hotel, Vrbo's tendency to attract longer stays is like a mini vacation for hosts. Guests on Vrbo often book week-long or even month-long stays, meaning fewer back-to-back cleanings and less wear-and-tear from constant check-ins and check-outs.

Longer stays don't just reduce your workload—they also mean higher revenue stability. When a guest books for an entire month, it's a win-win: they get a "home away from home," and you get to enjoy predictable income without the endless scramble for new bookings. Plus, you can offer discounts for longer stays to make your listing even more enticing. A week-long booking with a slightly reduced nightly rate still beats a bunch of one-nighters any day of the week.

## Owner Direct Communication: Building Relationships, One Message at a Time

Vrbo allows more direct communication between hosts and guests, which is a rare gem in the world of short-term rentals. Unlike some platforms (cough Airbnb cough), where messaging feels like it's monitored by Big Brother, Vrbo lets you chat with potential guests before they even book.

This level of interaction is a goldmine for building trust and rapport. You can answer questions, address concerns, and reassure guests that your property is exactly what they're looking for. And once they've had a great experience, you're more likely to see them again. Relationships built through direct communication can lead to repeat bookings—and who doesn't love a loyal guest who comes back year after year, always remembering to leave a stellar review?

### Key Takeaways: Vrbo's Unique Perks for Hosts

Vrbo isn't just another booking platform; it's a tailored tool for hosts who want to stand out and attract groups, families, and longer-term guests. By leveraging its user-friendly interface, direct communication features, and focus on whole-home rentals, you can create a strategy that's both profitable and manageable. It's like finding the perfect pair of jeans—comfortable, flattering, and full of pockets to stash all your hosting wins. So, go ahead, embrace the cool aunt energy of Vrbo, and make your rental the life of the vacation party.

## Booking.com: The Double-Edged Sword of Global Reach and Guest Chaos

When it comes to global reach, Booking.com is the undisputed heavy-weight champion. Think of it as the international megaphone for your property—blasting your listing to travelers in nearly every corner of the world. From business executives in Tokyo to backpackers in Berlin, everyone knows Booking.com. It's the platform where your listing can shine on a global stage and where you'll finally be able to say, "Oh, I have guests from everywhere!" But as with all great power, this comes with great... frustration.

The good news? Booking.com is designed to maximize your visibility like no other. Their search algorithms prioritize relevance, meaning your beautifully staged vacation home or quirky little cottage gets in front of the right eyeballs. Add in their promotional tools—like discounts, Genius programs, and seasonal campaigns—and your property gets even more love. It's like having a glitter cannon go off on your listing every time someone searches for a stay in your area.

The bad news? This glitter cannon comes with some serious cleanup. Guest cancellations are much more frequent on Booking.com than on platforms like Airbnb. Why? Because Booking.com doesn't require guests to pay a deposit or even provide much commitment up front. It's the digital equivalent of reserving a table at a fancy restaurant and ghosting them when you decide pizza sounds better. For hosts, this lack of accountability can feel like a gut punch—especially when you've held dates for weeks, only to have someone cancel at the last minute. It's not uncommon to see guests treat Booking.com like a "just in case" safety net while they lock in more secure plans elsewhere.

And then there's the guest communication...or lack thereof. Many guests use Booking.com like a vending machine: they press a button (or click "Book Now") and expect their room to pop out, ready to go, with minimal interaction. This can make building rapport challenging, especially for hosts who pride themselves on personalized touches or who like to know if their guests will need extra towels or a heads-up about the neighborhood rooster's 5 AM wake-up call.

## Promotional Tools: Discounts, Deals, and the Fine Art of Not Giving Away the Farm

Booking.com loves a good discount. In fact, they love it so much that they've turned offering promotions into an art form—or maybe a subtle form of arm-twisting. Their promotional tools are like a buffet of deals, each designed to make your listing more appealing to potential guests. Discounts for early bookers? Check. Last-minute deals? Check. Weekly and monthly rates? Double check. And don't forget the Genius program, where guests who've booked enough times get access to special discounts (10%, 15%, and 20%, depending on how generous you're feeling—or how much Booking.com pressures you).

At first glance, it all sounds great. More visibility? Yes, please! But here's where the fine print comes in, and things get a little dicey. Some discounts stack—meaning if you're not careful, your "generous" 10% discount could snowball into a jaw-dropping 35% once the Genius discount, early booker offer, and that random mobile user discount are all added together. Suddenly, you're left wondering why you're hosting guests at bargain-bin prices while still paying Booking.com their commission.

And oh, the mobile discount—because apparently, guests booking on their phones deserve a better deal than those using a laptop? Then there's the country-specific discounts (which sound like a fun way to target international travelers until you realize your "charming lakeside retreat" is now offering 20% off to guests booking from Japan, Italy, and Australia all at once). It's like playing a game of Discount Jenga, and one wrong move could send your profitability crashing down.

To be fair, these promotional tools do work—if used strategically. They can increase your visibility and help fill your calendar during slow seasons. Offering a small discount might push hesitant guests to book, and highlighting unique features (like that quirky hot tub or pet-friendly policy) can set your listing apart from competitors. But here's the catch: Booking.com really wants you to opt in to these promotions. Their dashboard might as well have a blinking neon sign saying, "Offer discounts, or else!" It's not subtle. They'll remind you—frequently—that your ranking could be higher if only you'd agree to cut your prices a little more.

Promotional tools on Booking.com can be a blessing and a curse. Yes, they'll get you noticed, and yes, they can boost bookings—if you manage them carefully. But always read the fine print, double-check for stacking discounts, and remember: you're running a business, not a charity. Use these tools like you'd use hot sauce—sparingly, strategically, and never so much that it makes you sweat.

**Key Takeaway:** There's no denying the sheer power of Booking.co m's global audience. If you're looking to fill your calendar quickly, this platform is an absolute workhorse. It's the go-to choice for getting your property in front of thousands—if not millions—of potential guests. One click, and suddenly your listing is on the radar of a family planning a European vacation, a couple celebrating their anniversary in Bali, or a group of friends heading to the Alps. Global reach? Check. But as with all great power, there are a few quirks that come with it.

First off, you'll need to brace yourself for some serious high-maintenance moments. You'll be chasing down payments, navigating last-minute cancellations that make you want to scream into a pillow, and wondering if your listing has somehow transformed into the internet's "try-before-you-buy" section. It's like, one minute you're all set for a fully booked weekend, and the next, you're wondering why you're playing emotional ping-pong with a guest who cancelled for no good reason. Make sure to set your cancellation policy to 30 or 60 days to offset this because late cancellations are taking money out of your pocket.

Here's the real kicker: Booking.com doesn't let you make your own description. Yep, you read that right. You spend hours perfecting your listing, snapping the best photos, and writing a glowing description of your property, only for a mysterious algorithm to swoop in and create its own version of your "charming cottage" or "luxury villa." What does the algorithm come up with? Well, your guess is as good as mine! It's like someone grabbed your perfectly curated details and turned them into a generic, one-size-fits-all description. There's no "personal touch" here, just whatever the program spits out. At times, it feels like you're just along for the ride while Booking.com takes the wheel and drives your listing into unknown territory.

And let's not forget about those stacking discounts. This is where things can really get out of hand if you're not keeping a close eye on it. You might think you're offering a neat little 10% off deal, but by the time you factor in all the other discounts that magically get added—like that Genius member discount, the mobile discount, or the last-minute deal—you could find yourself offering 35% off without even realizing it. It's like you've stepped into a discount vortex, and suddenly your pricing strategy is holding on for dear life. But, at the same time, you can't ignore the fact that Booking.com brings in about 50% of my bookings, which makes it an essential tool in your hosting toolkit. So, despite the occasional chaos, it's hard to deny that this platform works—it just comes with a lot of extras you'll need to wrangle.

## Expedia: The 'Sleeper Hit' of Booking Platforms—With a Few Surprises

Expedia is like the quiet powerhouse of the booking world. It may not get as much love as Airbnb or Booking.com, but it's sneaky good—especially for hosts looking for something a little less chaotic. You see, Expedia's model is all about offering a seamless experience for both hosts and guests, and while it's often overshadowed by flashier competitors, it's got its own brand of charm that can work wonders for your property.

For starters, Expedia attracts guests who like to plan. If you're a host who enjoys a more predictable guest flow and appreciates a calm, collected guest booking experience, Expedia is your jam. They've got a loyal customer base of travelers who like their plans locked in—and they don't mind paying upfront. No last-minute "I'll cancel once I find something better" shenanigans here. Guests book, and they're committed. Sure, it's not as immediate as Booking.com or Airbnb, but when you get that booking, it's likely to stick.

And speaking of booking, Expedia also brings great visibility, especially if you're listing multiple properties. Their platform is like a "one-stop-shop" for vacationers, combining lodging with flights, car rentals, and even fun tours. Guests love that convenience factor—it's like Expedia is saying, "Why deal with ten tabs when you can do it all in one place?" That means when your property is featured, it's front and centre in a vacation-planning paradise. Who doesn't love a little extra attention when someone's planning the trip of a lifetime?

But here's the kicker: guest experience on Expedia can be downright stellar. They're known for a more personalized, curated experience, making guests feel like their booking is part of a larger vacation experience. If you're hosting a cozy cabin in the woods or a swanky beachside apartment, guests on Expedia might feel like they've stumbled upon a hidden gem (which, of course, they have!). By partnering with Expedia, you're not just offering a room or an apartment; you're giving guests an experience. Whether it's a last-minute booking or a week-long stay, they'll appreciate how easy it is to lock in those plans without getting bombarded by random pop-up windows or booking fees that make your head spin.

Now, like with any platform, there are a few quirks. Expedia does take a commission (obviously), and the platform's interface can feel a bit like using a vintage GPS—it gets you where you're going, but you may wonder how you ended up on a random dirt road once in a while. However, Expedia works hard to get you noticed, making it a solid platform to tap into for hosts who want to reach a wide range of travelers.

## Diverse Listing Options: The Buffet of Accommodations—Something for Everyone!

One of the best things about Expedia is its wildly diverse array of listings, making it feel like a buffet of options for guests—and a feast for hosts! Whether you've got a luxurious penthouse with panoramic views, a rustic cabin tucked away in the woods, or even a glamping setup with fairy lights and a tent that looks like something out of a Pinterest dream board, Expedia has a spot for you. They cater to all types of accommodations, which means no matter what your property looks like, there's a perfect market waiting for you.

This is particularly fantastic for hosts with unique or niche properties. Are you renting out a houseboat on a secluded lake, or maybe you've got a treehouse high above the ground with views that could make a grown person cry tears of joy? Well, Expedia thrives on properties that offer something different, so stand out by showcasing the special features of your space. These kinds of accommodations are like the exotic, off-menu items that make people look twice—and guess what? People love unique stays. Think about it: everyone's looking for that one-of-a-kind experience that'll give them stories to tell on Instagram. Expedia allows you to shine a spotlight on what makes your place extraordinary.

Not only does Expedia encourage you to list these eccentric, jaw-dropping spaces, but the platform also allows you to adapt and evolve based on what's hot. You'll get insights into current booking trends, so you'll know whether travelers are suddenly obsessed with tiny homes, or if they're flocking to pet-friendly rentals. This flexibility gives you the chance to pivot and adjust your offerings, tailoring your listings to match what people are actually looking for. Need to highlight your new rooftop garden or swanky home office for remote workers? Now you know how to attract the crowd. Plus, Expedia makes it easy to test different approaches, so you can experiment with what works best—because who doesn't love a little experimentation when it comes to turning a profit?

And it's not just about listing a cool space; it's about tapping into the growing segments of travelers that prefer certain types of stays. Whether you're catering to family reunions, business travelers, or solo adventurers—you can build your property's presence to attract the exact guests who will fall in love with your place. This means you get a better fit for your property and a higher chance of repeat bookings because you've put in the effort to create a listing that speaks to a specific traveller type. It's like dating: you wouldn't show up to a sushi date in a bowling alley—match your vibe to your audience!

In short, Expedia's platform gives you the freedom and flexibility to showcase your property exactly how it is—and helps you tap into the right crowd. Whether it's for a spontaneous weekend getaway or a month-long digital nomad retreat, there's a niche out there for everyone. And when your place is tailored to meet their needs, you'll see your bookings soar! Plus, all this variety makes you feel like you're on top of the world, offering a little something for everyone, while watching your calendar fill up like magic. What's better than that?

## Loyalty Programs: The Secret Sauce to Keeping Guests Coming Back for More!

Let's talk about loyalty programs—they're like the VIP club of the travel world, and Expedia knows how to roll out the red carpet. These programs offer guests incentives and rewards for their repeat bookings, which creates a pretty sweet deal for hosts. When guests rack up points for every booking, they feel like they're earning their way to the top tier of travel VIPdom, and trust us—they'll want to come back for more. It's a bit like when you go to your favorite coffee shop and they stamp your card—that feeling of getting closer to your reward just makes you more likely to return. Now imagine that, but with trips instead of coffee.

When guests are familiar with Expedia's rewards program, they're more inclined to prioritize listings that are a part of it. They get that warm, fuzzy feeling knowing they're earning points towards their next stay or that discounted weekend getaway. You know what that means for you, the host? Repeat guests! And repeat guests are like the golden retrievers of the rental world—loyal, predictable, and always happy to come back for more. These guests become staples in your calendar, providing that much-needed stability and predictability in your occupancy rates. They'll consistently book with you because they know the rewards and want to keep earning them.

But here's where it gets even better: you can get in on the action too. As a host, you can participate in Expedia's loyalty program and attract travelers who love a good bargain. This can be a real game-changer, especially if your space is suited for longer stays or repeat visits. When guests see that loyalty points can get them a deal on their next trip, it may just tip them in your direction—making your property the go-to spot for that budget-conscious, savvy traveller. Now, not only do you get repeat guests, but you're also the host of choice for deal-hunters looking for the best bang for their buck.

This kind of guest loyalty isn't just about securing bookings—it's about building a community of people who return year after year (or season after season), creating a solid stream of income for you. These guests often become your biggest promoters, telling their friends and family about your amazing rental, which means even more repeat bookings and a nice little word-of-mouth marketing boost.

## Key Takeaway

Expedia is a game-changer for hosts who want to tap into a global market while having the flexibility to showcase unique properties. From repeat guest loyalty to marketing muscle, integrated travel solutions, and the ability to be part of a broader travel experience, it offers a level of exposure and convenience that most other platforms just can't match. If you're looking for stability, visibility, and a bit of extra love for your unique property, then Expedia is definitely the platform you should consider adding to your short-term rental toolkit. It's got the right mix of global reach, flexibility, and guest loyalty to make your rental business thrive.

# Conclusion

Alright, we've covered the big hitters in the short-term rental world, but guess what? There's a whole jungle of platforms out there waiting for you to explore. From HomeAway to Agoda, the options are endless—like an all-you-can-eat buffet where you *could* pile your plate high... but should you?

Here's the deal: don't just sign up for every platform that exists like a kid in a candy store grabbing everything in sight. Sure, you *could* list on 15 different sites, but if you don't have a solid system in place, you'll be drowning in double bookings, mismatched rates, and a never-ending stream of guest messages. It's a recipe for chaos—like trying to host a dinner party where the oven, fridge, and dishwasher are all working against you.

The key? Be strategic. Pick a few strong contenders, get your automation tools in place, and make sure your calendar syncs like a well-oiled machine. That way, you can expand your reach without losing your sanity. Because trust me, there's nothing fun about waking up to five different booking confirmations for the same weekend.

**Here's a pro tip: You must sync your calendars. Because if you don't, get ready for the nightmare of double bookings, where you end up telling two guests "Sorry, no room at the inn" on the same night. That's the type of awkwardness that turns your hosting career into a trainwreck. Believe me, you do not want to find out the hard way that two guests have somehow managed to book your one-bedroom loft for the same weekend. It's like a bad reality show where you're the host, the producer, and the person frantically trying to figure out how to make it all work. And, spoiler alert: nobody wins when that happens.**

Now, let's talk about cancellations. The struggle is real, folks. You know how it is—guests cancel their bookings like it's a casual Tuesday afternoon, and suddenly you're looking at an empty calendar wondering where the "no-show" fairy went. But here's the kicker: every platform publishes the hosts who cancel, which is like adding insult to injury. You get penalized for cancellations, but meanwhile, the guests can cancel whenever they feel like it, (not quiet, they have to adhere to your cancellation policy, make sure you have one in place). But, as frustrating as it is, you've got to work with it. Just stay organized, keep your cool, and remember that you can't control everything—except your calendar sync and your ability to stay calm under pressure.

So, to wrap it up: pick the platforms that work for you, but don't go spread yourself too thin. Keep your calendar synced, be prepared for cancellations, and stay organized. Your future self will thank you when you don't have to run around like a chicken with its head cut off.

## Chapter Five

# Direct Bookings: Cutting Out the Middleman and the Drama

You've made it this far—time to grab a cocktail or coffee and discover my all-time favorite way to secure bookings: DIRECT

Direct bookings are the *secret weapon* every savvy short-term rental host should have in their toolkit. They're the VIP pass to your business, giving guests exclusive, front-row access to your property—no middlemen, no surprise fees, just pure, unfiltered hospitality on your terms. **This is by far the best way to get bookings.** Why? Because direct bookings put *you* in control. You're not at the mercy of some ever-changing algorithm, you don't have to fork over 15-20% in commission fees to a giant platform, and you can actually build **real relationships** with your guests instead of playing email tag through a third-party system. Plus, let's talk money. Direct bookings mean **more cash in your pocket**, and who doesn't love that? Instead of watching a chunk of your hard-earned income disappear into the black hole of platform fees, you keep more of the pie. And let's be honest, pie is delicious—you should get to enjoy *all* of it.

**Why Direct Bookings Are the Holy Grail of Hosting**

- **You're the boss.** No more bending over backward for platform policies that change every five minutes. You set the rules, the pricing, and the experience.

- **Lower fees = higher profits.** Instead of giving a cut to Airbnb or Vrbo, you can reinvest that money into making your property even better—or, you know, treating yourself to a well-earned spa day.

- **Better guest relationships.** Want to send a friendly reminder email or a personal "Welcome!" text? Go for it. When you control the booking process, you create a more personalized experience from start to finish.

- **Brand loyalty.** A guest who books directly with you is more likely to return, recommend your place, and become a repeat customer. Think of it like a favorite coffee shop—you go back because you love the experience, not because some app suggested it.

Now, I won't sugarcoat it—**getting direct bookings takes effort**. This isn't a "set it and forget it" situation like listing on Airbnb and waiting for their algorithm to do the heavy lifting. But here's the thing: **it's absolutely worth the investment**. Direct bookings put you in the driver's seat, give you higher profits, and allow you to create a **guest experience that's 100% yours**—no platform interference, no unexpected policy changes, no surprise fees slicing into your bottom line.

If you want to make **direct bookings a major part of your business strategy** (which you absolutely should), here's what you need to focus on the following:

## Craft a Drool-Worthy Website

**Think of Your Website as Your Rental's Online Dating Profile—Swipe Right on These Must-Haves!** Your website isn't just a place to collect bookings—it's your rental's first impression, its digital handshake, its way of saying, *"Hey there, traveler. You're going to love staying here."* Just like a great dating profile, it needs to look sharp, be easy to navigate, and scream *"book me now!"*

**Visual Feast: Make Your Property Irresistible:** People are *visual creatures*. Your listing could have the most charming, poetic description, but if your photos look like they were taken with a potato, guests are *not* going to be impressed. Your images should make them feel like they're already there, sipping coffee on the balcony or curling up in that impossibly cozy bed.

- **Use high-resolution images and videos**—no blurry, poorly lit shots that make your place look like a horror movie set.

- **Highlight your best features:** Got a dreamy reading nook? A ridiculously comfy-looking couch? A firepit where guests can toast marshmallows under the stars? Show it off!

- **Set the scene:** Think *cozy beds with layers of plush blankets*, *a sunlit patio perfect for morning coffee*, or *a dining table beautifully set for an Instagram-worthy brunch*. Make guests *feel* the experience before they even book.

- **Virtual tours = brownie points:** If a picture is worth a thousand words, a video is worth a million. A quick walkthrough video can turn curious browsers into instant bookings.

**Keep It Simple: Because No One Likes a Maze:** Ever been to a website where finding what you need feels like an escape room challenge? Yeah, don't do that to your guests. Your booking button should be **bold, bright, and impossible to miss**—like a neon "Open" sign at a late-night diner.

- **Make it front and center on every page.** Don't make guests hunt for it like it's hidden treasure.

- **Minimize booking steps.** If they have to jump through a bunch of hoops just to secure their stay, they might give up halfway through.

- **Secure, seamless payment.** Nothing screams *"run away"* like a checkout process that looks sketchy. Use a trusted processor like Stripe (low fees, super reliable) to keep transactions smooth and stress-free.

**Show Off Your Personality: Make Guests Feel at Home Before They Even Arrive:**Your website isn't just a booking portal—it's a reflection of *you*. People don't just book properties; they book experiences, and a little personality goes a long way.

- **Tell your story:** What inspired you to start hosting? What's unique about your space? A short, engaging *"About"* page makes your listing feel more personal.

- **Add a blog or FAQ section:** This isn't just for SEO juice (though, bonus points for that). It's a chance to share fun anecdotes, insider travel tips, or even wild hosting stories.

- **Inject some humor:** A little wit can make your website stand out. Example: *"Yes, the WiFi is fast enough for Zoom calls. No, we can't make your boss any less annoying."*

- **Local recommendations:** Guests love hosts who share the *good stuff*—those hidden-gem restaurants, the best sunset spots, and coffee shops that don't charge $7 for a latte.

## Bottom Line? A Killer Website = More Bookings & Happier Guests

Your website should be **pretty, practical, and packed with personality**. Nail those three, and guests won't just want to book—they'll *have* to. Because just like online dating, first impressions matter... and you want to be the one they choose, not the one they swipe left on.

**Go the Extra Mile**: Integrate guest testimonials directly into your website. Nothing says "book me" quite like glowing reviews from happy guests. Use quotes, photos, or even video snippets to build trust and excitement.

## Use a Website Management Platform That Does the Heavy Lifting

Building a website from scratch might sound about as fun as assembling flat-pack furniture without instructions. Luckily, there are platforms that handle the nitty-gritty for you, leaving you free to focus on what you do best—hosting!

**All-in-One Magic:** Many booking platforms, like Lodgify, come with a built-in website that includes a payment system, calendar syncing, and customizable templates. This means your calendar updates automatically whenever you get a booking from another source, saving you from the dreaded double-booking disaster.

**Effortless Setup:** Seriously, setting up a site on these platforms is so easy you could do it while binge-watching your favorite show. Choose a template, add your details, and voila—a professional website that'll make your property shine.

**Total Control:** Unlike traditional booking platforms, these systems let you manage reviews. That's right—no more sleepless nights over that one guest who complained about the weather. You decide which reviews appear, giving you the power to showcase your property in the best light.

**Lodgify Love:** I personally use Lodgify, and let me tell you, it's a game-changer. It's not just easy to launch but also looks incredible. The platform practically screams, "You're a pro!" Plus, guests will love how seamless and polished everything feels.

## If You're Not Using Lodgify, Here's What to Look Out For (Because Your Website Deserves Better Than a 2008 Vibe)

Let's face it: a janky, outdated website is about as appealing as a motel bedspread from the 80s. If you're managing your own bookings, your website needs to be slick, functional, and ready to wow. Here's what to keep in mind so your guests are rushing to book (instead of rushing to close the tab).

**Website Design Basics: Pretty, Fast, and Functional**

Your website is like the front door of your rental business. If it's ugly, confusing, or slower than a dial-up connection from 1998, no one's stepping inside—let alone handing over their credit card.

- **Keep it clean and clear:** A polished, modern design doesn't just look good—it screams, *"I'm a professional who has their life together!"* (Even if behind the scenes, you're running on coffee and last-minute to-do lists.) A sleek, easy-to-navigate site makes it simple for guests to find what they need without feeling like they're playing a game of Where's Waldo.

- **Be mobile-friendly:** Most people book trips while scrolling on their phones—probably in bed, probably at midnight, probably when they should be sleeping. If your site looks like a jumbled mess that requires Olympic-level pinching and zooming just to see the details, you are toast. No one has the patience for that.

- **Speed is key:** Slow load times are a one-way ticket to Bounce Town, population: your potential guests. Test your site speed regularly—because if it takes longer to load than it does to microwave a Hot Pocket, people are out.

## Integrated Booking Systems: "Take My Money" Made Easy

Your booking process should be so simple that a sleep-deprived, jet-lagged traveler could do it with one eye open. Because, let's be honest, some of your guests might not be tech wizards—and you don't want them rage-quitting mid-checkout.

- **Smooth and streamlined:** If your checkout process has more steps than a 12-part scavenger hunt, you're losing guests. Get them from browsing to booking in as few clicks as possible. No unnecessary forms, no distractions—just a straight shot to that "Book Now" button.

- **Instant confirmation:** Guests love the dopamine hit of a "You're booked!" email—it's the digital equivalent of a high-five. Don't make them wait in uncertainty. Nobody likes to sit around wondering if their booking actually went through or if they just threw money into the void.

- **Calendar magic:** Keep your availability up-to-date and synced across all platforms. Double bookings are the *oopsie-daisy* no host wants to make. "Oh, sorry, we actually rented this to someone else" is not the kind of customer service moment you want to have.

## Payment Processing: The Money Talk (Because That's Why We're Here, Right?)

Ah, payment—the part where guests officially commit and you finally get paid. Make it secure, easy, and guest-friendly, so they hand over their hard-earned cash with confidence.

- **Multiple options, please:** Credit cards? PayPal? Bank transfers? Crypto? Carrier pigeon with a bag of gold coins? (Okay, maybe not that last one.) But the more payment options you offer, the more people you can accommodate—just like a hipster coffee shop with 12 different milk alternatives.

- **Make it safe:** Your guests need to trust your payment system like they trust their grandma's cookie recipe. No sketchy checkout pages that scream "possible scam." Use a secure processor (I like Stripe—low fees, rock-solid reliability) and make sure guests feel 100% comfortable entering their payment info.

- **Clear pricing:** Nobody likes hidden fees sneaking up on them at checkout like a horror movie jump scare. Be upfront about costs—cleaning fees, security deposits, taxes—so your guests don't feel like they're being tricked. Transparency builds trust (and keeps those pesky chargebacks at bay).

## Essential Information: No Guesswork Allowed

Guests aren't mind readers, and they sure as heck don't want to dig for crucial details like they're on an archaeological expedition. Lay everything out nice and clear.

- **High-quality photos:** Blurry, dimly lit pics? Hard pass. Show your property in its best light—literally. Bright, professional-looking images make all the difference. If your place is gorgeous but your photos make it look like a haunted house, you've got a problem.

- **Engaging descriptions:** Your property isn't *just* a house or apartment—it's a *cozy retreat*, a *chic escape*, or a *serene getaway with a sunlit living room perfect for lazy mornings and Instagram-worthy breakfasts.* Sell the experience, not just the square footage.

- **Cancellation policies:** Be clear, be fair, and save yourself (and your guests) from future drama. No one likes last-minute cancellations, but making your policies straightforward helps prevent those *"Wait, I can't get a refund?!"* moments.

**FAQs**: Answer common questions before they're even asked. It's like psychic customer service.

**Key Takeaways:** Your website isn't just a digital brochure—it's the heart of your direct booking strategy. A clean design, seamless booking process, secure payment options, and all the right info will make your site a booking powerhouse. The bottom line? Treat your website like a 5-star guest. Make it beautiful, easy to navigate, and impossible to ignore. Because in the battle for bookings, the host with the best website wins.

## Utilizing Social Media for Direct Engagement: Because Your Property Deserves to Go Viral (In a Good Way)

Think of social media as your digital megaphone—except instead of shouting into the void, you're strategically charming potential guests into booking your place. Used correctly, social media isn't just about posting pretty pictures; it's about building relationships, establishing trust, and turning casual scrollers into paying guests.

Let's break down how to make your social presence work for you (and not just be another thing you "should probably post on").

## Choosing the Right Platforms: Know Where Your Guests Hang Out

Not all social media platforms are created equal—especially when it comes to vacation rentals. The goal isn't to be everywhere; it's to be where your potential guests are.

Instagram & TikTok: Perfect for stunning visuals, behind-the-scenes tours, and fun, engaging content. If your property has aesthetic vibes and photogenic corners, these platforms are your best friends.

Facebook: Great for community building and running ads. Plus, your aunt is probably already on there, sharing cat videos, so why not turn it into a booking machine?

Pinterest: An underrated gem for travel inspiration. A solid pin with "Dreamy Beachfront Escape" can live on forever and drive direct traffic to your site.

LinkedIn: Okay, this one's a stretch unless you're renting out an executive retreat space. But hey, no judgment if you want to flex your hosting business here!

**Pro Tip: Collaborate with influencers and travel bloggers who align with your brand. A well-placed "Weekend Escape" post from the right person can get your inbox blowing up with inquiries.**

## Engaging Content Creation: Because Boring Doesn't Sell

If your social media presence is just a handful of random posts saying, "Book now!"—we need to talk. Social media is about storytelling, not spamming.

**Show, Don't Tell:** High-quality photos and videos of your property in action are a must. Think cozy morning coffee shots, sunset balcony views, or a guest popping champagne in your hot tub (safely, of course).

**Guest Testimonials**: A glowing review is great, but a video of a guest saying, "This was the best weekend getaway ever" while sipping wine on your patio? Even better.

**Behind-the-Scenes:** Show what goes into making your rental amazing—cleaning hacks, restocking the welcome basket, or even a funny blooper reel of things that go wrong (like that one time the decorative pillows refused to cooperate).

**Contests & Giveaways**: Want engagement? Offer a free night's stay or a discount for people who share your post. Suddenly, your followers turn into your unpaid marketing team.

**Pro Tip: Not a natural on camera? No worries—your property is the star. Just give it a little personality.**

## Building a Community: More Than Just Likes and Follows

A strong social media presence isn't about racking up numbers—it's about actual engagement. Guests who feel connected to your brand are more likely to book (and rebook).

**Talk to Your Followers**: Respond to comments, answer DMs, and make people feel heard. Nothing builds loyalty like a friendly, engaged host.

**Encourage User-Generated Content:** Ask guests to tag your rental in their posts and repost their photos (with permission). Their vacation memories = free marketing for you.

**Create a VIP Club:** A private Facebook or Instagram group for past guests? Genius. You can share exclusive deals, early access to bookings, and special perks, making them feel special while keeping them coming back.

**Pro Tip: Make social interactions feel personal. A guest who got a friendly response from you today might be a direct booking next month.**

## Promotions & Offers: Because Everyone Loves a Good Deal

Let's be honest—people love feeling like they're getting an exclusive deal. Social media is the perfect place to drop limited-time promos and special discounts.

**Use Clear CTAs**: Every post should have a purpose. "Click the link to book," "DM for a special rate," or "Use code VIPSTAY for 10% off"—make it easy for guests to take action.

**Create Urgency**: "Only 2 weekends left at our special winter rate!" Suddenly, people who were thinking about booking feel the FOMO and pull the trigger.

**Exclusive Discount Codes:** Reward your social media followers with special offers. A little "Thanks for following! Here's a secret deal just for you" goes a long way.

**Pro Tip: Make it feel exclusive. Even if it's a 5% discount, calling it a "Secret Follower Rate" makes it way more enticing.**

**Key Takeaways:** Social media isn't just for scrolling and posting cute dog videos (though, let's be real, that's a solid 80% of it). Used strategically, it's a powerful tool to build relationships, boost engagement, and drive direct bookings.

✔ Choose the right platforms—don't waste time where your guests aren't.

✔ Create engaging, visual content that makes people want to stay at your property.

✔ Foster a sense of community—people book from brands (and hosts) they trust.

✔ Leverage promotions and exclusive deals to drive direct bookings.

The bottom line? If you're not using social media to engage guests and boost bookings, you're leaving money on the table. And nobody likes leaving money on the table.

## The Importance of Email Marketing Campaigns: Sliding Into Inboxes the Right Way

Email marketing isn't just for spamming people with "exclusive" deals on overpriced gym memberships. When done right, it's one of the most powerful tools to keep guests engaged, grow your brand, and drive direct bookings. Think of it as a cozy little conversation you're having with your potential and past guests—except you don't need to pick up the phone (thank goodness).

Here's how to nail email marketing without making people hit "unsubscribe faster than you can say 'promo code.'"

**Building an Email List**: Because Who Doesn't Like a VIP Club?

Your email list is gold. It's like having a private audience who's already shown interest in what you're offering. But how do you build this treasure trove?

**Ask (Nicely):** "Sign up for our newsletter!" is boring. Try: "Be the first to know about exclusive offers, dreamy getaways, and secret discounts!" Give people a reason to join—like 10% off their next booking or a free guide to the best local spots.

**Keep It Fresh**: Regularly update your list to make sure it's filled with real, engaged people. No one needs emails bouncing back or sitting unread in ancient inboxes.

**Segment Like a Pro**: Not all guests are created equal. Some want romantic getaways, while others are planning family reunions (and need way more towels). Tailor your emails based on interests and booking history—it's like matchmaking for marketing.

**Pro Tip: Make sign-ups easy. Pop-ups, website forms, and even a "Sign Up" checkbox at checkout can work wonders.**

## Crafting Compelling Newsletters: Make Them Actually Want to Read It

Newsletters don't have to be boring walls of text with a "BOOK NOW" button slapped on the bottom. The goal is to entertain and inform while keeping your property top-of-mind.

**Property Updates:** Did you just redecorate? Add a hot tub? Finally fix that squeaky door? Share it! Guests love knowing your property is always improving (and ready for Instagram).

**Local Flavour**: Highlight upcoming events, attractions, or festivals near your property. "Stay with us and enjoy the annual Lobster Festival!" sounds a lot better than, "Hey, we're still here."

**Guest Stories:** Have a guest who had an amazing experience? Share their testimonial or photos (with permission, of course). It's the ultimate social proof.

**Special Offers:** Everyone loves a deal. Include exclusive discounts, last-minute openings, or flash sales—but make them feel like a gift, not a sales pitch.

**Pro Tip: Keep it short and visually appealing. Nobody wants to read a novel in their inbox. Use headers, bullet points, and plenty of gorgeous images.**

**Automated Campaigns: Because Time Is Money**

You don't have to send every email manually (unless you really enjoy staring at your inbox). Automation is your secret weapon for keeping communication consistent and efficient.

**Welcome Emails:** A quick "Thanks for subscribing! Here's a little something for your next stay" sets the tone for a warm relationship. Bonus points if it includes a discount or helpful travel tips.

**Special Occasion Emails:** Wish guests a happy birthday, anniversary, or just a "Hey, it's been a year since your last visit—come back and see us!" These personal touches can turn casual guests into loyal ones.

**Abandoned Bookings:** Someone started booking but didn't finish? Send a friendly reminder: "Your dream getaway is waiting! Finish your booking now and save 5%." FOMO works wonders.

**Pro Tip: Use humor and charm in your automated emails. Nobody wants to feel like they're talking to a robot.**

**Analyzing Results: Because Guessing Doesn't Cut It**

Sending emails is one thing—knowing if they're working is another. Track your performance like it's the final season of your favorite show.

**Open Rates**: Did they even read it? If not, your subject line might need a little spice. "Book Now!" is boring. "Your Next Dream Vacation Awaits..." is intriguing.

**Click-Through Rates**: Are people actually clicking the links? If not, maybe your offer isn't clear enough—or your buttons are hiding like Waldo.

**A/B Testing**: Test different subject lines, layouts, or content to see what works best. It's like experimenting in the kitchen, but with fewer dishes to clean.

**Ask for Feedback:** A quick survey can tell you what guests love (and don't love) about your emails. Plus, it shows you care.

**Pro Tip: Don't overdo it. Emailing every day = annoying. Emailing once or twice a month with valuable content = genius.**

**Key Takeaways**

Email marketing isn't about spamming inboxes—it's about building relationships. Done right, it's a powerful way to stay connected with guests, promote your property, and keep those bookings rolling in.

✔ Build a list of engaged guests with irresistible incentives.

✔ Send newsletters that people actually want to open.

✔ Use automation to save time and stay consistent.

✔ Analyze your campaigns so you can improve and refine.

The bottom line? Emails aren't dead—they're alive and thriving. So go ahead, slide into those inboxes with style, charm, and a touch of humor.

## The Direct Booking Love Affair: Why It's the Best Relationship You'll Ever Have

Direct bookings are the *holy grail* of short-term rentals. They're like dating someone who actually texts back, listens to your needs, and doesn't demand an expensive dinner (*looking at you, OTA platforms with your 15-20% commission fees*). When guests book directly, **you're in control**—no middleman taking a chunk of your hard-earned money, no third-party rules dictating how you communicate, and no mystery fees creeping in like an unwanted subscription service. Instead, you get to **build real relationships** with your guests, tailor their experience, and keep them coming back. And let's talk about **data ownership**—because, yes, it matters! With direct bookings, you actually get your guests' contact info (*with permission, of course*) so you can send them thoughtful reminder emails, welcome texts, and maybe even a special discount for their next stay. Compare that to OTA platforms, where your guests' details are locked away like a top-secret government file. Oh, and the money? **Let's talk about the money.** Instead of waving goodbye to 15-20% of your earnings just for existing on a platform, you're only paying a measly **1.6% to Stripe.** That's barely the cost of an iced coffee. Would you rather give up hundreds of dollars per booking, or just one overpriced latte? I think we both know the answer. At the end of the day, **direct bookings are a win-win**. Guests get a personalized, seamless experience, and you get full control over your business, your profits, and your guest relationships. It's the best kind of relationship—one that's built on trust, value, and absolutely no commission-guzzling third parties.

So, if you're not prioritizing direct bookings yet, **what are you waiting for?** Your business (and your bank account) will thank you.

# Chapter Six

# Setting Up for Success: Branding and Marketing

Whether its an amazing pool or something else, your property has something special so let's talk about how to highlight it.

Building a memorable brand and crafting a killer marketing strategy is like creating the perfect cocktail—a mix of creativity, strategy, and a little dash of "wow factor." A strong brand identity doesn't just look good; it screams, "Stay here and love it." It's not just about logos and catchy taglines—it's about creating an experience that sticks with your guests long after they've left. Your brand should make them feel something, whether it's cozy comfort, luxurious indulgence, or adventurous wanderlust. Here's how to create a brand that makes your guests' booking fingers twitch, a marketing strategy that turns browsers into buyers, and a vibe that keeps them coming back for more.

Think of your brand as the personality of your rental business. It's the look, the feel, and the story you're telling. It's what makes someone say, "I want to stay there," rather than scrolling past your listing. And your marketing? That's the megaphone that amplifies your brand's message to the world. Together, they're your dream team for attracting guests, building loyalty, and boosting bookings.

## Designing an Attractive Brand Identity: It's Not Just a Logo, It's a Vibe

## Establishing a Unique Brand Voice: Be Memorable, Not Meh

Your brand voice is the personality of your rental business. Is it warm and welcoming? Luxurious and aspirational? Quirky and fun? Nail it down, and let it shine.

- Connect on a Personal Level: A unique voice can make your emails, social media posts, and listing descriptions feel like a chat with an old friend—the kind you want to visit.

Your brand's voice is the bridge between you and your guests. It's what makes your communication warm, engaging, and relatable. Instead of sounding like a corporate robot, infuse your personality into everything you do. Imagine you're writing to your best friend—someone you genuinely care about and want to impress.

- **Emails:** Instead of a generic "Thank you for booking" email, try something like, "We're so excited to host you! Get ready for cozy nights, stunning views, and memories you'll treasure."

- **Social Media Posts:** Share behind-the-scenes glimpses of your property or quirky updates about your rental journey. Guests love seeing the human side of your business.

- **Listing Descriptions:** Paint a vivid picture. Instead of "Spacious 2-bedroom with amenities," say, "Relax in our sunny living room with floor-to-ceiling windows, perfect for sipping morning coffee or unwinding after a day of exploring."

When your communication feels personal, guests feel valued—and that's a feeling they won't forget.

**Stand Out in the Crowd: No one remembers the generic host who "has Wi-Fi and a comfy couch." They remember the one who says, "Unwind with a glass of wine on our sunset-soaked terrace."**

In a sea of rentals, being unique is your ticket to standing out. Guests scroll through countless listings every day—make yours the one they stop on.

- **Highlight What's Special:** Do you have a killer view, a quirky design feature, or a historic charm? Lean into it! For example, "Our rental is nestled in a 19th-century barn that's been lovingly restored into a modern retreat."

- **Add Personality:** Use language that's true to your vibe. If your rental is luxurious, opt for phrases like "opulent escape." If it's cozy, try "a snug retreat."

- **Create a Visual Hook:** Pair your unique descriptions with stunning photos that tell the same story. If you're pitching "sunset-soaked terraces," show off a shot of golden hour with a glass of wine on the table.

Guests don't just want a place to stay; they want an experience. Make yours unforgettable, and they'll be hitting that "Book Now" button in no time.

### Consistency is Key: Whether you're on Instagram or sending a booking confirmation, your voice should be unmistakably you.

Consistency across all your channels builds trust and makes your brand feel cohesive. Think of it like your rental's personality—guests should recognize you anywhere they encounter you, whether it's an Instagram Reel, a welcome email, or a handwritten thank-you note.

- **Stay True to Your Style:** If your brand is fun and quirky, don't switch to formal and stiff in your emails. Keep the tone consistent everywhere.

- **Visual Consistency Matters Too:** Use the same fonts, colors, and logo across your website, social media, and print materials. Guests should be able to recognize your brand at a glance.

- **Reinforce Your Brand Story:** Consistently share bits of your story. For example, if your property is a family-run business, weave that narrative into your content—whether it's photos of your family helping out or posts about why you started hosting.

When your brand feels cohesive and authentic, guests are more likely to trust you. And trust? That's the foundation of every great booking relationship

## Creating a Logo and Visual Elements: Your Property's Signature Look

Your logo is the face of your brand, and your visuals—colors, fonts, imagery—are its wardrobe. Make it count.

- **Instant Recognition:** A great logo sticks, like a catchy tune you hum all day. Think simple, sleek, and memorable.

- **Cohesive Design:** Use the same visuals across your website, social media, and even your in-unit welcome guide. Consistency builds trust.

- **Professional = Credible:** A DIY logo made on a free app? No thanks. Invest in something polished—it shows guests you're serious.

## Crafting a Compelling Brand Story: Tell the Tale, Sell the Stay

### People Love Stories—So Share Yours!

People love stories, especially ones that make them feel something. A compelling narrative helps guests relate to your brand on an emotional level, creating trust and excitement about booking your space.

### Be Relatable: Make Your Story Personal

Why did you start hosting? What makes your property special? Maybe it's the reclaimed wood dining table with a rich history or the lavender you planted by hand that fills the air with a relaxing scent. Share the journey that led you to open your doors to guests—whether it was a lifelong dream, a family tradition, or an unexpected adventure. Personal details make your story memorable and give guests a reason to choose *you* over a faceless corporate rental.

### Create Connection: More Than Just a Place to Stay

Your story isn't just about your property—it's about the experiences it creates for your guests. A family celebrating their first big vacation, a couple enjoying a romantic getaway, or a solo traveler finding peace in a new place. Show them how your space fosters memories, whether it's morning coffee on the balcony with a breathtaking sunrise or cozy movie nights by the fireplace. Emotional connections make guests feel like they're part of something special, not just renting a place to sleep.

## Boost Engagement: Make Your Brand Feel Human

A great story makes your brand feel more human, which encourages people to hit that "book now" button. When potential guests see genuine passion behind your listing, they're more likely to trust and engage with you. Use storytelling in your:

- **Website and Listings:** Paint a picture of what guests can expect, not just with features, but with experiences.
- **Social Media Posts:** Share snippets of your hosting journey, behind-the-scenes moments, or fun guest stories (with permission, of course).
- **Email Marketing:** Instead of generic promotions, weave stories into your newsletters—like the time you helped a honeymooning couple make their stay extra special.

The more authentic and engaging your storytelling, the stronger your brand becomes. People remember stories far more than a list of amenities, so use yours to leave a lasting impression.

**Defining Your Target Audience: Don't Try to Be Everything to Everyone**

Knowing who you're marketing to is half the battle. Focus on your ideal guests, and watch your bookings soar.

- **Who Are They?:** Families? Couples? Solo adventurers? Identify their demographics and needs.
- **Tailor Your Efforts:** Market differently to honeymooners looking for romance and digital nomads who just want strong Wi-Fi and good coffee.
- **Get Personal:** When you know your audience, you can speak directly to them. It's like writing a love letter... but for bookings.

## Leveraging SEO for Better Visibility: Let Google Do the Heavy Lifting

Being searchable online is the modern-day equivalent of being listed in a "Best Places to Stay" travel guide. Here's how to rank like a pro.

### Keyword Research: Speak Your Guests' Language

Keywords are what guests type into search engines, so make sure you're speaking their language.

- **Find the Magic Words:** Use tools like Google Keyword Planner, Uber suggest, or SEMrush to find terms like "charming lakefront cabin" or "luxury city apartment rental." These are the words and phrases people are already searching for—use them to your advantage.

- **Understand Search Intent:** Are guests looking for a weekend getaway or a long-term stay? Cater to their needs in your descriptions. If someone searches "cozy winter cabin for couples," they're expecting a romantic, snug experience—so make sure your listing highlights the fireplace, plush blankets, and scenic snowy views.

- **Be Strategic:** Sprinkle those keywords throughout your website, blog, and listings like salt on fries—just enough to be tasty, not overwhelming. Overstuffing your listing with keywords can feel unnatural and off-putting to readers (and search engines).

## Optimizing Your Property Descriptions: Sell the Experience

SEO isn't just about keywords; it's about *how* you use them. Your descriptions should read naturally and enhance the guest experience.

- **Engaging and Descriptive:** Instead of saying, "This apartment has a great view," write, "Wake up to panoramic city skylines and sip your morning coffee as the sunrise bathes the room in golden light."

- **Keyword Integration:** Weave keywords in organically—mention nearby attractions, amenities, and experiences your property offers without making it sound robotic.

- **Format Matters:** Use bullet points, bold text, and short paragraphs to make your listing easy to skim. Guests (and Google) love clear, well-structured content.

## Utilizing Local SEO Strategies: Own Your Location

Your guests aren't just looking for a place to stay—they're looking for an *experience.* Use local SEO to help them find you.

- **Mention Local Attractions:** Reference nearby hotspots like "5-minute walk to the beach" or "a stone's throw from the city's best coffee shops."

- **Use Location-Specific Keywords:** "Best vacation rental in Miami," "cozy cabin near Yellowstone," or "beachfront Airbnb in Malibu" can help boost your visibility.

- **Create Local Content:** Blog about nearby events, restaurant recommendations, or hidden gems in your area to draw in potential guests searching for travel tips.

## Building Backlinks: Boost Your Credibility

A solid backlink strategy can significantly increase your website's authority and search ranking.

- **Partner with Travel Bloggers & Influencers:** Getting featured on travel websites or in social media posts can generate valuable backlinks.

- **Collaborate with Local Businesses:** Cross-promote with nearby restaurants, tour guides, and local attractions. "Stay at our rental and get 10% off at Joe's Café" is a win-win for everyone.
- **Guest Blogging:** Write for travel blogs, short-term rental industry websites, or local tourism pages and include a link back to your site.

## Final Thoughts: Get Seen, Get Booked

SEO isn't just about algorithms, analytics, and confusing jargon—it's about making sure your *perfect* guests can actually find you when they're searching for a place to stay. Think of it as putting a giant neon sign on the internet that says, **"Hey, this is the vacation rental you've been looking for!"** Without proper SEO, your website is just another hidden gem that nobody knows exists.

When done right, SEO helps your **listing climb the search ranks, attract more visitors, and, most importantly, drive more direct bookings**. The best part? Once you've optimized your website effectively, Google does a lot of the heavy lifting *for you*. Instead of relying on paid ads or hoping for word-of-mouth, your website will naturally appear when potential guests search for accommodations in your area.

But here's the thing—SEO isn't a "set it and forget it" kind of deal. It requires **consistency, strategy, and a little patience**. From using the right keywords (the ones your guests are actually searching for) to making sure your website loads at lightning speed, every little tweak helps push your ranking higher. The goal? To get your rental in front of the right audience *before* they end up clicking on an Airbnb or Vrbo listing.

So, start optimizing, start ranking, and let Google work its magic while you focus on what you do best—**delivering an unforgettable guest experience that keeps them coming back for more.** Because at the end of the day, the more visible your site is, the more bookings you'll secure, and the less you'll have to rely on third-party platforms that eat away at your profits.

## Creating Professional Photography for Listings: Make Them Stop Scrolling

Guests shop with their eyes. Professional photos are your best chance to make them pause and think, "I *have* to stay here."

## Investing in Professional Photography: Because iPhone Pics Don't Cut It

- **First Impressions Count:** Professional photos can be the difference between a full booking calendar and tumbleweeds in your inbox.
- **Sell the Space:** Photographers know how to capture light,

angles, and composition to make your property shine.

- **ROI Guaranteed:** One great photo can pay for itself with a single booking.

### Highlighting Key Features: Show Off What Makes You Special

- **Focus on the Good Stuff:** Got a clawfoot tub? A firepit? Killer views? Make sure they're front and center.
- **Tell a Story:** Your photos should show guests what their experience will look like—relaxing by the pool, cooking in the gourmet kitchen, or curling up by the fireplace.
- **Cover All Angles:** Include wide shots, close-ups of charming details, and both interior and exterior views.

### Utilizing Staging Techniques: Make It Pinterest-Worthy

### Set the Scene: Transform Your Space into a Dream Stay

First impressions matter, and your rental should invite guests to imagine themselves living their best lives. Fluff those pillows, light a candle, and set the table with stylish dinnerware. Consider adding fresh flowers or a book on the coffee table to create an inviting ambiance. The goal is to make the space feel effortlessly chic yet welcoming.

### Less Is More: Keep It Clean and Clutter-Free

Nobody books a place that looks like a yard sale. A minimalist approach works best—remove unnecessary items, leaving only intentional decor that enhances the space. Guests should feel like they're stepping into a well-designed, peaceful retreat rather than sorting through personal belongings. Every piece should serve a purpose and contribute to the overall aesthetic.

### Add Personality: Little Touches, Big Impact

It's the little things that make a big difference. A few well-placed props—like a tray with coffee and croissants, a stylish throw blanket, or a welcome note—can make your space feel more inviting. Personalized details, such as a local travel guide or a basket of snacks, show thoughtfulness and elevate the guest experience.

## Incorporating Diverse Angles and Lighting: The Secret Sauce

### Play with Angles: Highlight the Best Features

Show off the layout and make small spaces look bigger with creative perspectives. Wide-angle shots work well for capturing entire rooms, while close-ups can highlight charming details like textured walls, cozy reading nooks, or unique design elements. Experiment with different viewpoints to create a visually dynamic gallery that truly showcases your property's potential.

### Light It Right: Use Natural Light to Your Advantage

Natural light is your BFF when it comes to creating bright, inviting photos. Shoot during the golden hour—just after sunrise or before sunset—for a warm, dreamy glow that enhances the space. If natural light is scarce, use soft artificial lighting to keep things looking warm and inviting rather than harsh and sterile.

### Show It All: Capture Different Moods and Times of Day

Guests want to envision their entire stay, from waking up to a sunny morning to cozying up at night. Capture different lighting scenarios—daytime for airy brightness, night time for a moody ambiance, and even rainy days for a cozy retreat vibe. A well-rounded gallery creates a more immersive experience for potential guests, helping them picture their stay from start to finish.

By mastering staging techniques and leveraging angles and lighting, you create a visual experience that makes your rental stand out in a crowded market. A well-staged, beautifully lit space isn't just photogenic—it's *bookable*.

### Key Takeaways: Your Brand Is Your Booking Magnet

Building a memorable brand and crafting a killer marketing strategy is like creating the perfect cocktail—a mix of creativity, strategy, and a little dash of "wow factor." A strong brand identity doesn't just look good; it screams, "Stay here and love it." It's not just about logos and catchy taglines—it's about creating an experience that sticks with your guests long after they've left. Your brand should make them feel something, whether it's cozy comfort, luxurious indulgence, or adventurous wanderlust. Here's how to create a brand that makes your guests' booking fingers twitch, a marketing strategy that turns browsers into buyers, and a vibe that keeps them coming back for more.

Think of your brand as the personality of your rental business. It's the look, the feel, and the story you're telling. It's what makes someone say, "I want to stay there," rather than scrolling past your listing. And your marketing? That's the megaphone that amplifies your brand's message to the world. Together, they're your dream team for attracting guests, building loyalty, and boosting bookings.

Creating a strong brand and executing smart marketing isn't rocket science, but it does take effort. From crafting a killer logo to mastering SEO and showcasing jaw-dropping photos, every piece works together to build trust, attract guests, and drive those glorious direct bookings. It's about making a promise to your guests—that their stay will be everything they dreamed of and more—and delivering on it, every time. Your brand is your handshake, your hello, your "welcome home," and your marketing is the spotlight that ensures the world sees it.

So go ahead, create a brand that's unforgettable, a marketing strategy that's unstoppable, and photos that make people say, "Take my money!" Lean into your creativity, be bold in your storytelling, and never underestimate the power of a polished, personal touch. Your rental business isn't just a listing; it's a destination, an experience, and a memory waiting to happen. With the right branding and marketing, you're not just hosting—you're building something extraordinary.

## Short-Term Rental Property Setup Guide

### Essential Amenities Checklist

- Comfortable, high-quality bedding & pillows
- Extra towels & linens
- Fast & reliable Wi-Fi
- Basic kitchen essentials (pots, pans, utensils, plates, cups, etc.)
- Coffee maker & supplies (coffee, tea, sugar, creamer)
- Basic toiletries (shampoo, conditioner, soap, toothpaste)
- Smart TV or streaming device
- Heating & air conditioning controls
- Iron & ironing board
- Hairdryer
- First-aid kit
- Laundry access (washer/dryer, detergent)

## Interior Design & Furnishing Guide

- Choose a cohesive color scheme
- Use high-quality, durable furniture
- Invest in blackout curtains for bedrooms
- Provide comfortable seating in living areas
- Use stylish but functional storage solutions
- Add cozy rugs and throw blankets
- Decorate with local art or unique decor pieces
- Ensure good lighting (ambient, task, and accent lighting)
- Create a welcoming entryway with hooks & storage
- Keep decor minimal but warm and inviting

## Guest Experience Enhancements

- Welcome guide with house rules & local recommendations
- Complimentary snacks or welcome basket
- Detailed check-in & check-out instructions
- Streaming service subscriptions or cable TV

- Books, board games, or entertainment options
- Blackout curtains & white noise machine for restful sleep
- Flexible check-in/check-out options when possible
- Clear & friendly communication before and during stay
- Personalized touches (handwritten notes, seasonal decor, etc.)

## Tech & Automation for Efficiency

- Smart locks for self-check-in
- Security cameras (exterior only) for safety
- Noise monitoring devices to prevent disturbances
- Smart thermostat for energy efficiency
- Automated messaging system for guest communication
- Online guidebook with house rules & local recommendations
- Backup power sources (portable charger, generator if needed)
- Digital concierge service (QR code for recommendations)

## Safety & Compliance Must-Haves

- Smoke & carbon monoxide detectors in key areas

- Fire extinguisher in kitchen
- Emergency exit plan displayed
- Proper insurance for short-term rentals
- Compliant with local zoning & licensing regulations
- Childproofing if hosting families (outlet covers, safety gates, etc.)
- Well-lit entryways & secure locks
- No-slip mats in bathrooms & high-traffic areas

This checklist ensures your STR is fully equipped, stylish, and optimized for guest satisfaction and operational efficiency! By focusing on high-quality amenities, thoughtful interior design, seamless guest experiences, smart automation, and essential safety measures, you can create a welcoming and memorable space that keeps guests coming back. A well-prepared rental not only enhances guest comfort but also improves your ratings and increases profitability. Investing time and effort into these key aspects will set your STR apart, ensuring long-term success in the competitive short-term rental market!

Chapter Seven

# The Weird and Wonderful World of Booking.com

Ah, Booking.com—a platform so big it's like the Kmart of the travel world. Love it or hate it, you can't ignore it. And let me tell you, I **do not** love it. In fact, I've tried to quit it several times, but guess what? **50% of my bookings now come from this platform.** It's like that one friend who always shows up uninvited, eats all your snacks, and somehow convinces you they're indispensable.

While their host service might feel non-existent (seriously, don't hold your breath waiting for a helpful support call unless you enjoy hearing hold music from another century), their reach is enormous. They bring in guests from places you didn't even know existed. If you're not on Booking.com, you're potentially missing out on a *huge* pool of guests. But like any powerful tool, you've got to know how to use it—and avoid cutting yourself in the process. Because trust me, if you're not careful, Booking.com will have you bleeding money, patience, and possibly your will to live.

The quirks? Oh, they are *plentiful.*

- Their website looks like it was designed in the early 2000s and never updated.

- Don't even get me started on their backend. Trying to work out what you will be paid and when or what booking you have is a challenge and I am being kind.

- Their support team is based in Singapore, and they assume you're running a 200-room hotel with a front desk, accounting department, and a dedicated guest services team.

- Your listing gets randomly distributed across obscure third-party sites, so guests will occasionally book your property through a site you've never heard of, and they'll show up expecting something completely different.

But despite all the things that drive me *absolutely bonkers* about B ooking.com, I have to give credit where it's due: they deliver bookings. They're a guest-generating machine, particularly during the off-season when Airbnb and VRBO might not be pulling their weight. And in a business where cash flow is king, I can't afford to ignore them. So, I begrudgingly continue to list my properties there, knowing that with the right approach, I can make it work for me instead of against me.

Booking.com is like that weird uncle who gives you great birthday presents but also insists on telling you conspiracy theories at family gatherings. It's a mixed bag, but if you learn how to navigate the chaos, you can make it work in your favor. Just be prepared for some *unusual* guest interactions, questionable last-minute bookings, and the occasional technical nightmare. But hey—if it fills your calendar and keeps the income flowing, it's a relationship worth maintaining.

## Booking.com: My Experience

I have several properties listed on Booking.com, and while it's not my favorite platform to work with, it does have its advantages—especially in the off-season. If you're in an area with a consistent climate year-round, Booking.com can be a great way to fill those slower months when other platforms might not bring in as many guests.

That being said, **the support team is largely based in Singapore**, which means when you call them, they often assume you're running a massive hotel operation rather than being a single property owner or a small business. I've had my fair share of frustrating conversations where they ask me to "contact my accounting department" or "check with my front desk team"—as if I have either! Be prepared for some miscommunication and a lot of patience.

Another quirk of Booking.com is that your property will end up on **many smaller partner websites** you've never even heard of. More than once, I've had guests book a stay at one of my properties through a completely random website I had no idea my listing was on. While this can be good for exposure, it can also make it tricky when guests arrive confused, thinking they booked through a different company altogether.

Short-term rentals are a **fantastic** way to earn income, but let's be honest—**not all platforms operate the same way, and not all guests are created equal**. Each platform has its quirks, and if you're not prepared, you might find yourself dealing with **confused guests, last-minute bookings, or some truly head-scratching situations.**

## Here are a couple of common pitfalls to watch out for—and how to avoid them like a pro.

### Guests Who Don't Read Instructions

**The Problem:** Unlike Airbnb and Vrbo guests, **Booking.com users seem to have an allergy to reading check-in instructions**. No matter how clearly you spell things out in your automated messages, you'll still get frantic calls like:
"Where's the address?" (It was sent in three different emails.)
"How do I get in?" (The check-in code was in bold, underlined, and possibly even sung by a choir.)
"What time is checkout?" (The same time listed on the website, in the messages, and on the **big sign in the living room.**)

**How to Avoid It:**

**Triple your communication.** Send check-in details via email, text, and platform messages. (And maybe consider skywriting.)

**Use visuals!** A simple graphic or a short video walkthrough of the check-in process can reduce confusion.

**Keep it fool proof.** If possible, set up self-check-in so guests can't claim they "missed" the key handover instructions.

**Expect last-minute questions.** Have a standard, copy-paste response ready so you're not retyping the same thing at midnight.

## Instant Booking Free-for-All (Booking.com's Open-Door Policy)

**The Problem:** Unlike Airbnb, where hosts can require guest verifications and pre-approve bookings, **Booking.com operates like an all-you-can-eat buffet—anyone can book, instantly, no questions asked.** This can be **nerve-wracking** if you prefer to screen guests before they show up at your front door. Imagine waking up to a last-minute booking for **tonight** from someone with no prior reviews, no profile photo, and an email address that looks suspiciously like "guest12345@definitelynotascammer.com." Yeah, **Booking.com doesn't vet guests for you**—so that's on you.

**How to Avoid It:**

**Manually confirm bookings when possible.** Set your settings to require at least **24 hours' notice** before a guest can check in.

**Require a security deposit.** If someone isn't willing to put down a small refundable deposit, that's a red flag.

**Use a guest screening service.** Services like Autohost or Superhog can help verify identities before arrival.

**Have a solid cancellation policy.** If you get a gut feeling about a booking, don't be afraid to enforce stricter rules to protect your property.

## Who Are The guests?: No Guest Review System = Total Mystery Guests

Unlike Airbnb, Booking.com has **no feedback system for hosts to review guests.** That means you have absolutely no idea who is turning up to stay in one of your most valuable assets. It's a bit like playing accommodation roulette—you're either getting a wonderful, respectful traveler *or* a guest who thinks your home is an all-you-can-take buffet.

I know a host who accepted a late-night booking, only to wake up the next morning and find that the guest had helped herself to *everything*—and I mean **everything**. I'm talking coffee machine, every towel and sheet, duvet covers, pillows, you name it. Even the soap. **THE SOAP.**

This wasn't a case of someone accidentally packing a towel in their suitcase—it was a full-scale heist. And what did Booking.com do about it? **Absolutely nothing.** The host reported the theft, hoping for some form of support or compensation, only to receive the standard **"We're sorry, but we're just a booking platform"** response.

Without a guest review system, there's no way to flag bad guests for future hosts, which means someone who stole an entire linen closet from one property can just go book another stay without consequence. Hosts are left in the dark, hoping the next guest doesn't walk off with their furniture.

## How to Protect Yourself from Mystery Guests

Since Booking.com won't let you screen guests via reviews, here are some ways to safeguard your property:

### 1. Require Prepayment and a Security Deposit

Make sure guests are putting down money before they arrive. If Bo oking.com allows you to opt into their payment collection system, **do it.** Otherwise, require prepayment or a hefty security deposit before handing over check-in details. If someone doesn't want to put down a deposit, that's a red flag.

### 2. Install a Smart Lock with ID Verification

No more handing over keys blindly. Use a **smart lock** that requires guests to upload an ID before check-in. If a guest refuses to do this, it might be time to reconsider their booking.

### 3. Keep Valuables Locked Away

If you have high-end appliances, decor, or items that you *really* don't want to see disappear, keep them locked away or out of guest reach. Some hosts even go as far as installing **locked storage closets** for extra linens and valuables.

### 4. Have Clear House Rules and Cameras at Entry Points

Make sure guests know your rules upfront, especially regarding **unauthorized visitors, damages, and theft.** Cameras at entry points (not inside the property) can also help deter guests with sticky fingers.

### 5. Get Insurance Specifically for Short-Term Rentals

Some platforms offer host protection, but Booking.com? Not so much. Look into **proper short-term rental insurance** that covers theft, damages, and those "oops, I took your coffee machine" moments.

- **Payments Are a Gamble:** Unlike Airbnb and VRBO, Book ing.com does *not* automatically collect payments for all properties. Some listings qualify for payment processing, but for others, you have to **request** to be part of their payment collection program. In the beginning, I assumed they were handling payments for all my properties—only to have two guests stay without ever paying because I hadn't set up a manual collection process!

- **Tax Confusion:** Booking.com does not handle tax payments on your behalf, which is very different from Airbnb and VRBO. Taxes are included in your payout, and it's *your* responsibility to ensure they are paid to the correct authorities.

- **Fee Collection Hassles:** Instead of deducting their commission from your payouts like Airbnb and VRBO, Booking.com sends you an invoice **one month later** and expects you to manually pay it. If you forget, they'll start limiting the visibility of your listings—something that can seriously impact your bookings if you're not keeping track.

## How to Leverage Booking.com's Enormous Reach

- **Use It as a Supplement, Not Your Only Platform:** Booking.com is a fantastic *additional* tool for visibility, but I would never recommend relying on it as your sole booking platform. It's best used alongside Airbnb, VRBO, and direct bookings.
- **Adjust Your Pricing to Cover Fees:** Their commission fees are significant, so build them into your nightly rates to avoid eating into your profits.
- **Ensure Your Calendar is Synced:** Booking.com does *not* make it easy to update availability manually. I highly recommend using a **channel manager** to sync all your calendars across platforms to prevent double bookings.
- **Prepayment is Key:** If you're eligible for Booking.com's payment collection program, enroll in it. Otherwise, **require prepayment** to avoid guests staying without paying (yes, it happens!).
- **Prepare for More Hands-On Guest Communication:** Because Booking.com guests often don't read instructions, you'll need to be proactive in reminding them about check-in details and house rules.
- **Watch Out for No-Shows:** Since Booking.com doesn't re-

quire guests to confirm or verify much before booking, you may experience a higher rate of no-shows compared to other platforms. Having a clear cancellation policy can help mitigate this risk.

## Stories from the Trenches: A Host's Survival Guide

To give you an idea of what you might encounter, here are some real-life experiences from hosting on Booking.com in Australia:

- **The Ghost Booking:** I once had a guest book a two-week stay, never show up, and completely ghost me. Because they never canceled, I wasn't able to rebook those dates, and since I hadn't required prepayment at the time, I didn't get paid. Lesson learned: always require prepayment or have a strict cancellation policy in place.

- **The "Surprise" Extra Guests:** Another time, a guest booked for two people but showed up with six. When I explained that the listing clearly stated a maximum of two guests, they were shocked—apparently, they booked through a third-party partner site that hadn't listed the occupancy limits correctly. Now, I double-check my listing across all connected platforms regularly.

- **The Midnight Call:** One time, a guest called me at **midnight** asking for check-in instructions, even though I had sent them multiple messages. They had booked last-minute, hadn't read anything, and assumed there would be a 24-hour front desk. Now, I make sure to emphasize in my listing that it's a *self-check-in* property.

## How to Survive Booking.com Without Losing Your Sanity

If you're going to use Booking.com, you need to know how to *handle* Booking.com—otherwise, you'll be crying into your morning coffee wondering why you ever signed up in the first place. Here are some tried-and-true survival tips:

### 1. Have a 30 or 60-Day Cancellation Policy

Trust me on this. If you let guests cancel last-minute without penalty, you'll have people ghosting you left and right. Unlike Airbnb, which generally encourages fair policies, Booking.com guests seem to have an uncanny ability to book and cancel faster than you can refresh your inbox. If you want to avoid the heartbreak of lost revenue, set a **firm** cancellation policy—preferably **30 to 60 days**—so that guests have skin in the game before they hit that "book now" button.

### 2. Opt into Booking.com Collecting Payments on Your Behalf

This one is *huge.* Booking.com has an option where they collect payments for you, but **you have to call them and ask to be included**—it's not automatic. If you don't do this, you'll have to manually chase payments from guests, and trust me, that is **not** a fun experience. I once had a guest stay for five nights and disappear without paying, and I had assumed Booking.com was handling it. (Spoiler alert: they weren't.) Do yourself a favor and **opt-in ASAP.**

### 3. Double-Check Your Discounts—Because They STACK

Booking.com is notorious for encouraging hosts to apply discounts, but what they *don't* tell you is that many of them **stack** on top of each other like a discount Jenga tower. A 10% Genius discount plus a 15% mobile discount plus a 20% last-minute deal? Congratulations, you just gave someone a **45% off stay** without realizing it. Always check your settings, test your listing as if you were a guest, and be very selective about which discounts you opt into.

### 4. Sync Your Calendar or Regret It Later

## Trying to Cancel a Booking.com Guest is a Host's Worst Nightmare

Trying to cancel a Booking.com guest due to a double booking is like trying to escape quicksand—you struggle, you stress, and the more you fight it, the worse it gets. Not only do they refuse to let you cancel without penalty, but they'll take it upon themselves to find "alternative accommodation" for your guest. Sounds great, right? Wrong. **If that**

**accommodation is more expensive, you are paying the difference.** Yes, you read that right.

Imagine a guest books your **$150-per-night** rental, and due to a double booking, Booking.com swoops in like a vengeful ex and decides to relocate them to a **$400-per-night luxury resort.** Guess who's covering that unexpected upgrade? YOU. You may as well roll out the red carpet, hand them a complimentary bottle of champagne, and personally fan them with a palm leaf while they sip cocktails by the infinity pool—because you're footing the bill for their five-star experience.

Now, you might be thinking, *"Surely, they'll find them something within the same price range?"* HA! Booking.com operates on the "not our problem" principle, so if the only available accommodation is the Ritz-Carlton, then guess what? You're now sponsoring an unsuspecting guest's dream vacation. And no, you don't get a thank-you card.

## How to Avoid This Money-Sucking Black Hole

### 1. Sync Your Calendar Like Your Life Depends on It

Double bookings are **the** number one way to fall into Booking.com's cancellation nightmare, so do yourself a favor and **sync your calendars properly.** If you're manually updating availability across multiple platforms, you may as well be playing Russian roulette with your business. **Use a channel manager** or a **direct API integration** to make sure all your listings are speaking to each other in real-time.

If you're relying on **iCal sync**, brace yourself—it doesn't update instantly, which means you're always at risk of a double booking. iCal operates on a delay, sometimes up to **a few hours** (which in the world of instant bookings might as well be a lifetime). In that time, a guest could book your space on Airbnb, and before the sync catches up, another guest books the same dates on Booking.com. Boom. **Now you have two guests expecting the same bed.** Have fun sorting that out.

The **best** way to avoid this nightmare is to invest in a **proper booking platform or channel manager** that syncs in real-time. Yes, it might cost a little, but trust me—it's cheaper than sending a guest to a five-star hotel on your dime.

## 5. Be Prepared for the Worst Customer Support of Your Life

Calling Booking.com's support is like yelling into the void. They have a knack for misunderstanding basic requests, putting you on hold for eons, and then responding with, "We will get back to you"—which they rarely do. If you have an issue, brace yourself for frustration and try to solve it yourself before wasting hours on hold. Better yet, join host forums and Facebook groups where other Booking.com survivors share their wisdom.

## Final Thoughts: Tame the Beast, Don't Let It Eat You

Booking.com is **not** for the faint of heart—it's like the wild west of short-term rental platforms, complete with **unexpected twists, ag-**

**gressive pricing tactics, and the occasional guest who treats your place like a hotel with 24/7 concierge service.** But if you approach it with **strategy, patience, and a healthy dose of scepticism**, it can be an *incredible* source of bookings that fills your calendar and boosts your revenue.

Here's the deal: **Booking.com plays by its own rules**—and if you're not careful, you might find yourself tangled in a web of surprise policies, frustrating pay-out delays, and guest expectations that don't always align with short-term rental hosting. (**Pro tip: Some guests think they're booking a full-service hotel. Spoiler alert: They are not.**)

## Survival Tips for Navigating Booking.com Like a Pro

- **Set firm boundaries.** Booking.com loves to default to flexible cancellation policies, instant bookings, and automatic discount offers. If you're not careful, you'll wake up to a new booking that comes with a 10% discount *you didn't even approve.*

- **Read the fine print.** And then read it again. Booking.com's terms are like a tricky puzzle—you think you've got it figured out until a random policy pops up and surprises you. *Know what you're agreeing to before you hit "publish."*

- **Double-check everything.** Rates, cancellation policies, deposit requirements—Booking.com doesn't always make it easy to adjust settings, so triple-check that everything is exactly how you want it before you start accepting guests.

- **Be prepared for last-minute bookings.** Unlike Airbnb, where guests usually plan ahead, Booking.com guests love to book at the *last second*. If you're not ready to handle someone checking in **tonight**, make sure you adjust your availability settings accordingly.

- **Watch out for the "Pay at Property" setting.** This little gem means you might end up with a booking where the guest is supposed to pay you directly on arrival—except sometimes they just...don't show up. If you'd rather avoid the "no-shows" and payment chases, opt for prepaid bookings.

## The Bottom Line? Go In With a Plan—Or Risk Bookin g.com Purgatory

Booking.com *can* be a powerful tool in your rental business, but **it's not a set-it-and-forget-it platform**. If you just throw your listing up and hope for the best, you might find yourself in **Booking.com purgatory, wondering where it all went wrong, drowning in last-minute reservations, and chasing guests for payments that should've been collected automatically.** But if you take control—**set strict policies, adjust your settings carefully and stay on top of your listings**—it can be a **lucrative** addition to your short-term rental strategy. Just remember: **This isn't Airbnb. This isn't Vrbo. This is Booking.com, and you need to play smart.**

To sum it up:

**Sync your calendar properly** with a real-time tool, not just iCal.

**Opt into Booking.com collecting payments on your behalf** so you don't have to chase guests for money.

**Check your discounts regularly** so you don't accidentally end up giving guests a free stay. Only use discounts when you have to and make sure they work for you. Check what you are offering and when because you have to opt out of dates rather than opt in.

**Set a firm cancellation policy** (30-60 days) to avoid last-minute no-shows.

**Always have a backup plan**—because Booking.com sure won't have one for you.

For me, the key to making Booking.com work is using it as a secondary platform rather than my main source of bookings. If you're willing to adapt and stay on top of the platform's quirks, it can help bring in those much-needed off-season guests and expand your reach beyond the usual Airbnb and VRBO crowd. With safeguards in place, you can enjoy the **benefits** of Booking.com (because, let's face it, they do bring bookings) while avoiding most of the **headaches** that come with it. And most importantly—you won't be sending guests to luxury resorts on your own dime.

## Chapter Eight

# The Underdogs—VRBO, Expedia, and Other Platforms That Deserve a Spot in Your Toolkit

While Airbnb and Booking.com may dominate the short-term rental conversation, there's a whole world of **smaller but mighty platforms** that can bring in valuable bookings. Platforms like **VRBO, Expedia, Agoda, and TripAdvisor** may not get as much attention, but they absolutely have their place in a well-rounded hosting strategy. Each of these platforms has its quirks, pros, and cons, and learning how to **leverage them correctly** can add a steady stream of extra income to your business.

Now, before you start wondering if I'm about to list **every single booking channel out there**, let me stop you. If I tried to write a chapter on all of them, this book would turn into an encyclopedia so heavy you'd need a dolly just to carry it around. Seriously, there are **dozens** of booking platforms globally—some that cater to specific regions, others focused on niche markets like pet-friendly rentals or eco-conscious travelers. While they each have their merits, I've chosen to focus on the **biggest hitters** beyond Airbnb and Booking.com: platforms that I've personally worked with and know can make a real difference to your bottom line.

Think of these platforms as the supporting actors in the blockbuster movie that is your hosting business. They may not take center stage, but their roles are crucial in filling your calendar, diversifying your bookings, and reaching audiences you might not otherwise attract. Whether it's **VRBO for families, Expedia for business travelers, or TripAdvisor**

**for tourists**, these platforms can help you build a more resilient and profitable rental business.

Let's dive into these **smaller but essential players** and how you can make them work for you.

## VRBO: The Airbnb Alternative for Longer Stays & Family Bookings

VRBO (Vacation Rentals by Owner) has been around *forever* (since 1995, actually), and while it doesn't have the same massive guest traffic as Airbnb, it has a dedicated base of travelers—mainly **families, groups, and people looking for longer stays.**

### How VRBO is Different from Airbnb

**No Shared Spaces** – VRBO only allows whole-property rentals, so no renting out that spare bedroom like on Airbnb.

**Higher-Quality Guests** – The average VRBO guest is looking for a vacation home, not a cheap one-night stay, so you generally get **fewer party risks** and more responsible travelers.

**Longer Bookings** – VRBO guests tend to book longer stays, which means **fewer turnovers** and more stability.

**Lower Fees** – VRBO takes **fewer commissions** than Airbnb, making it a more profitable platform per booking.

### VRBO Hosting Tips

**Set Weekly & Monthly Discounts** – Since VRBO attracts **longer-stay guests,** offering weekly or monthly discounts can push your listing higher in search results and bring in solid bookings.

**Highlight Family-Friendly Features** – If you have **cribs, high chairs, board games, or a fenced backyard,** mention it! VRBO families love those little details.

**Encourage Direct Bookings** – VRBO allows **direct guest communication,** making it easier to build relationships and encourage repeat bookings outside the platform.

**Have a Strict Cancellation Policy** – VRBO guests book further in advance than Airbnb travelers, so having a **strict cancellation policy** protects you from last-minute dropouts.

**Use Professional Photos** – VRBO guests expect a **home-like experience,** so great photos of cozy bedrooms, family spaces, and outdoor areas can increase bookings.

## A VRBO Host Story

A host I know in Sydney switched to VRBO after dealing with too many **one-night party guests on Airbnb.** Within three months, she had **three separate 30-day bookings,** all from families looking for extended stays. Less cleaning, less hassle, and **WAY** more money. Now, she only takes **5+ night bookings** and is making more than she ever did with Airbnb

## Expedia & Its Network: Hidden Gems for More Bookings

Expedia may not be the first place you think of when listing a short-term rental, but it should be. Unlike Airbnb or VRBO, Expedia is part of a massive network that extends far beyond just one booking site. When you list your property on Expedia, it doesn't just appear on their site—it gets distributed **across multiple high-traffic partner websites** including **Hotels.com, Travelocity, Orbitz, Wotif, CheapTickets, and Hotwire.** Essentially, you're getting your property showcased on a collection of travel booking giants without having to create multiple listings manually.

Think of Expedia as **a one-stop shop for guest visibility**—particularly for business travelers, international tourists, and last-minute bookers who are used to booking hotels but are increasingly looking at vacation rentals as an alternative. Many travelers browsing these sites **aren't even searching for short-term rentals specifically**, but when they see a well-presented listing in the mix, they may be tempted to book a stay at your property instead of a hotel.

Another major advantage of Expedia's network is **its strong reputation in the travel industry.** Many travelers trust Expedia and its partner sites because they've been booking flights, hotels, and car rentals with them for years. This built-in trust factor can make potential guests **more likely to book your rental**, particularly if they've never used platforms like Airbnb or VRBO before. Additionally, since Expedia's audience often consists of **business professionals, event attendees, and corporate travelers**, you're reaching a market segment that tends to book longer stays, is less likely to cancel last-minute, and is more inclined to treat your property with respect.

While Expedia's rental listings still play second fiddle to its hotel offerings, there is a growing demand for short-term rentals on the platform. And since **most hosts don't think to list their properties on Expedia**, competition is significantly lower than on Airbnb or Booking.com. This means you have a better chance of getting **higher visibility and better placement in search results**, leading to more potential bookings with less competition.

By listing on Expedia, you're not just tapping into a **single** booking platform—you're unlocking access to an entire ecosystem of travel websites. If you're looking to **expand your guest pool, diversify your sources of bookings, and target a new category of travelers**, Expedia is a platform worth considering.

## Why I Use Them In Short

**Good for Urban & Business Travelers** – Many Expedia guests are booking stays for **work trips, events, or conferences.**

**No Guest Reviews to Worry About** – Unlike Airbnb, you don't have to worry about **getting a five-star rating every time.**

**Competitive Pricing Algorithms** – Expedia has smart pricing tools that help you stay competitive without constant manual adjustments.

## Expedia Hosting Tips

**Set Business-Friendly Amenities** – Wi-Fi, work desks, and self-check-in options can **attract corporate travelers** looking for a hassle-free stay.

**Offer Discounts for Longer Stays** – Business travelers often need **a week or more**, so setting up a discount for stays of **7+ nights** can boost bookings.

**Be Flexible with Check-In & Check-Out** – Many Expedia guests are **coming from flights,** so flexible arrival times can help secure more bookings.

**Optimize Your Listing for Multiple Platforms** – Since Expedia distributes listings across **multiple partner sites,** make sure your photos, descriptions, and pricing look great on all platforms.

## An Expedia Host Story

A Melbourne host who listed on Expedia as an experiment was shocked to find her property **fully booked within a month**—mostly by **corporate guests and travelers flying in for conferences.** Since then, she has added more business-friendly amenities (like express check-in, a printer and keyless entry) and now gets a steady flow of midweek bookings, **filling the gaps between her weekend Airbnb stays.**

## TripAdvisor Rentals: The Power of Reviews for More Bookings

TripAdvisor may be best known for restaurant reviews, but it also has a **vacation rental division** that many hosts overlook. If you have a property with **great reviews**, TripAdvisor can be an absolute **goldmine for extra bookings**—especially from international travelers who rely heavily on user feedback when planning their trips.

One of TripAdvisor's biggest advantages is its **built-in credibility**. Many travelers already use TripAdvisor to research their destinations, read restaurant reviews, and plan excursions. If they're already on the platform **checking out the best places to visit**, why wouldn't they also book a stay through it? Having a **highly-rated property on TripAdvisor Rentals** means you can catch these travelers right when they're planning their trip.

Another reason TripAdvisor Rentals can be a powerful tool is its **SEO strength**. Because TripAdvisor is one of the most visited travel sites in the world, listings on the platform often show up higher in **Google search results** than those on other booking platforms. This means a well-optimized listing with great reviews has **a better chance of being seen by travelers** actively searching for accommodations in your area.

Additionally, TripAdvisor **ranks listings based on reviews**, meaning that the more positive feedback you get, the higher your property will appear in search results. Unlike Airbnb or Booking.com, where algorithms are constantly changing and favoring different factors, **TripAdvisor's ranking system is largely review-driven**—making it a platform where good service and guest experience can genuinely **translate into better visibility and more bookings.**

TripAdvisor Rentals also has a strong **international audience**, particularly among European travelers who are accustomed to using TripAdvisor for trip planning. If you're looking to attract more global guests, **having a listing here can be a great way to diversify your bookings** beyond just domestic travelers.

## How to Succeed on TripAdvisor Rentals

**Encourage Happy Guests to Leave Reviews** – Since TripAdvisor is **review-driven**, positive ratings can significantly improve your ranking and increase your visibility.

**Use Local SEO in Your Description** – Mention local landmarks, attractions, and popular activities near your rental. Guests searching for those places will be more likely to discover your listing.

**Offer Unique Experiences** – TripAdvisor travelers love **one-of-a-kind stays**. If your property has something unique—whether it's a scenic rooftop, a historical background, or exclusive local insights—highlight it in your listing.

**Highlight Your Best Reviews in the Description** – Guests scrolling through listings tend to skim details, so pulling a standout review or two into your listing's main description can grab their attention.

**Keep Your Listing Active & Updated** – Frequently updating your listing, adjusting pricing, and responding to guest inquiries quickly can help improve your ranking within TripAdvisor's search results.

## A TripAdvisor Host Story

A host in Byron Bay decided to list their beachfront rental on TripAdvisor, thinking it wouldn't make much of a difference. Within a few months, they noticed **a steady stream of bookings from interna-**

**tional travelers**, particularly from Europe. Turns out, their property was appearing **at the top of Google searches for "best places to stay in Byron Bay"**—all because TripAdvisor's SEO game is that strong. Now, 50% of their bookings come from TripAdvisor, simply because their property ranks high in search results, thanks to **glowing reviews from past guests**.

## Final Thoughts: Should You Use These Platforms?

**If you want to diversify your bookings and reduce Airbnb dependence, YES.**

**If you're tired of Airbnb's constant changes and policies, YES.**

**If you want fewer party guests and more families or corporate travelers, YES.**

Each of these platforms has its **own strengths and audience**, and using them strategically can help fill your calendar, reduce risk, and boost profits. The beauty of these "underdog platforms" is that they allow you to **diversify your bookings** in a way that makes your business more resilient. By listing your property across multiple sites, you're opening the door to different types of guests—families on VRBO, business travelers on Expedia, and international vacationers on TripAdvisor.

It's important to remember that no single platform can serve all your needs. While Airbnb and Booking.com might bring in the majority of your bookings, these secondary platforms can fill the gaps and create a well-rounded, stable stream of income. Think of it like an investment portfolio—you wouldn't put all your money into one stock, so why rely on just one booking channel?

So, whether it's **VRBO for longer stays, Expedia for business travelers, or TripAdvisor for high-rated vacation rentals**, these platforms could be your secret weapon for **better, more stable bookings**. By optimizing your listings for their unique audiences, you're not only reaching more potential guests, but you're also ensuring that your short-term rental business remains profitable and adaptable no matter what changes come your way.

While Airbnb and Booking.com may dominate the short-term rental conversation, there's a whole world of **smaller but mighty platforms** that can bring in valuable bookings. Platforms like **VRBO, Expedia, Agoda, and TripAdvisor** may not get as much attention, but they absolutely have their place in a well-rounded hosting strategy. Each of these platforms has its quirks, pros, and cons, and learning how to **leverage them correctly** can add a steady stream of extra income to your business.

Now, before you start wondering if I'm about to list **every single booking channel out there**, let me stop you. If I tried to write a chapter on all of them, this book would turn into an encyclopaedia so heavy you'd need a dolly just to carry it around. Seriously, there are **dozens** of booking platforms globally—some that cater to specific regions, others focused on niche markets like pet-friendly rentals or eco-conscious travelers. While they each have their merits, I've chosen to focus on the **biggest hitters** beyond Airbnb and Booking.com: platforms that I've personally worked with and know can make a real difference to your bottom line.

Think of these platforms as the supporting actors in the blockbuster movie that is your hosting business. They may not take center stage, but their roles are crucial in filling your calendar, diversifying your bookings, and reaching audiences you might not otherwise attract. Whether it's **VRBO for families, Expedia for business travelers, or TripAdvisor for tourists**, these platforms can help you build a more resilient and profitable rental business.

Let's dive into these **smaller but essential players** and how you can make them work for you.

## VRBO: The Airbnb Alternative for Longer Stays & Family Bookings

VRBO (Vacation Rentals by Owner) has been around *forever* (since 1995, actually), and while it doesn't have the same massive guest traffic as Airbnb, it has a dedicated base of travelers—mainly **families, groups, and people looking for longer stays.**

### How VRBO is Different from Airbnb

**No Shared Spaces** – VRBO only allows whole-property rentals, so no renting out that spare bedroom like on Airbnb.

**Higher-Quality Guests** – The average VRBO guest is looking for a vacation home, not a cheap one-night stay, so you generally get **fewer party risks** and more responsible travelers.

**Longer Bookings** – VRBO guests tend to book longer stays, which means **fewer turnovers** and more stability.

**Lower Fees** – VRBO takes **fewer commissions** than Airbnb, making it a more profitable platform per booking.

## VRBO Hosting Tips

**Set Weekly & Monthly Discounts** – Since VRBO attracts **longer-stay guests,** offering weekly or monthly discounts can push your listing higher in search results and bring in solid bookings.

**Highlight Family-Friendly Features** – If you have **cribs, high chairs, board games, or a fenced backyard,** mention it! VRBO families love those little details.

**Encourage Direct Bookings** – VRBO allows **direct guest communication,** making it easier to build relationships and encourage repeat bookings outside the platform.

**Have a Strict Cancellation Policy** – VRBO guests book further in advance than Airbnb travelers, so having a **strict cancellation policy** protects you from last-minute dropouts.

**Use Professional Photos** – VRBO guests expect a **home-like experience,** so great photos of cozy bedrooms, family spaces, and outdoor areas can increase bookings.

## A VRBO Host Story

A host I know in Sydney switched to VRBO after dealing with too many **one-night party guests on Airbnb.** Within three months, she had **three separate 30-day bookings,** all from families looking for extended stays. Less cleaning, less hassle, and **WAY** more money. Now, she only takes **5+ night bookings** and is making more than she ever did with Airbnb.

## Expedia & Its Network: Hidden Gems for More Bookings

### Expedia & Its Network: A Powerhouse of Booking Sites

Expedia may not be the first place you think of when listing a short-term rental, but it should be. Unlike Airbnb or VRBO, Expedia is part of a massive network that extends far beyond just one booking site. When you list your property on Expedia, it doesn't just appear on their site—it gets distributed **across multiple high-traffic partner websites** including **Hotels.com, Travelocity, Orbitz, Wotif, CheapTickets, and Hotwire.** Essentially, you're getting your property showcased on a collection of travel booking giants without having to create multiple listings manually.

Think of Expedia as **a one-stop shop for guest visibility**—particularly for business travelers, international tourists, and last-minute bookers who are used to booking hotels but are increasingly looking at vacation rentals as an alternative. Many travelers browsing these sites **aren't even searching for short-term rentals specifically**, but when they see a well-presented listing in the mix, they may be tempted to book a stay at your property instead of a hotel.

Another major advantage of Expedia's network is **its strong reputation in the travel industry.** Many travelers trust Expedia and its partner sites because they've been booking flights, hotels, and car rentals with them for years. This built-in trust factor can make potential guests **more likely to book your rental**, particularly if they've never used platforms like Airbnb or VRBO before. Additionally, since Expedia's audience often consists of **business professionals, event attendees, and corporate travelers**, you're reaching a market segment that tends to book longer stays, is less likely to cancel last-minute, and is more inclined to treat your property with respect.

While Expedia's rental listings still play second fiddle to its hotel offerings, there is a growing demand for short-term rentals on the platform. And since **most hosts don't think to list their properties on Expedia**, competition is significantly lower than on Airbnb or Booking.com. This means you have a better chance of getting **higher visibility and better placement in search results**, leading to more potential bookings with less competition.

By listing on Expedia, you're not just tapping into a **single** booking platform—you're unlocking access to an entire ecosystem of travel websites. If you're looking to **expand your guest pool, diversify your sources of bookings, and target a new category of travelers**, Expedia is a platform worth considering.

## Why I Use Them In Short

**Good for Urban & Business Travelers** – Many Expedia guests are booking stays for **work trips, events, or conferences.**

**No Guest Reviews to Worry About** – Unlike Airbnb, you don't have to worry about **getting a five-star rating every time.**

**Competitive Pricing Algorithms** – Expedia has smart pricing tools that help you stay competitive without constant manual adjustments.

## Expedia Hosting Tips

**Set Business-Friendly Amenities** – Wi-Fi, work desks, and self-check-in options can **attract corporate travelers** looking for a hassle-free stay.

**Offer Discounts for Longer Stays** – Business travelers often need **a week or more**, so setting up a discount for stays of 7+ **nights** can boost bookings.

**Be Flexible with Check-In & Check-Out** – Many Expedia guests are **coming from flights,** so flexible arrival times can help secure more bookings.

**Optimize Your Listing for Multiple Platforms** – Since Expedia distributes listings across **multiple partner sites,** make sure your photos, descriptions, and pricing look great on all platforms.

## An Expedia Host Story

A Melbourne host who listed on Expedia as an experiment was shocked to find her property **fully booked within a month**—mostly by **corporate guests and travelers flying in for conferences.** Since then, she has added more business-friendly amenities (like express check-in, a printer and keyless entry) and now gets a steady flow of midweek bookings, **filling the gaps between her weekend Airbnb stays.**

## TripAdvisor Rentals: The Power of Reviews for More Bookings

TripAdvisor may be best known for restaurant reviews, but it also has a **vacation rental division** that many hosts overlook. If you have a property with **great reviews**, TripAdvisor can be an absolute **goldmine for extra bookings**—especially from international travelers who rely heavily on user feedback when planning their trips.

One of TripAdvisor's biggest advantages is its **built-in credibility**. Many travelers already use TripAdvisor to research their destinations, read restaurant reviews, and plan excursions. If they're already on the platform **checking out the best places to visit**, why wouldn't they also book a stay through it? Having a **highly-rated property on TripAdvisor Rentals** means you can catch these travelers right when they're planning their trip.

Another reason TripAdvisor Rentals can be a powerful tool is its **SEO strength**. Because TripAdvisor is one of the most visited travel sites in the world, listings on the platform often show up higher in **Google search results** than those on other booking platforms. This means a well-optimized listing with great reviews has **a better chance of being seen by travelers** actively searching for accommodations in your area.

Additionally, TripAdvisor **ranks listings based on reviews**, meaning that the more positive feedback you get, the higher your property will appear in search results. Unlike Airbnb or Booking.com, where algorithms are constantly changing and favoring different factors, **TripAdvisor's ranking system is largely review-driven**—making it a platform where good service and guest experience can genuinely **translate into better visibility and more bookings.**

TripAdvisor Rentals also has a strong **international audience**, particularly among European travelers who are accustomed to using TripAdvisor for trip planning. If you're looking to attract more global guests, **having a listing here can be a great way to diversify your bookings** beyond just domestic travelers.

## How to Succeed on TripAdvisor Rentals

**Encourage Happy Guests to Leave Reviews** – Since TripAdvisor is **review-driven**, positive ratings can significantly improve your ranking and increase your visibility.

**Use Local SEO in Your Description** – Mention local landmarks, attractions, and popular activities near your rental. Guests searching for those places will be more likely to discover your listing.

**Offer Unique Experiences** – TripAdvisor travelers love **one-of-a-kind stays**. If your property has something unique—whether it's a scenic rooftop, a historical background, or exclusive local insights—highlight it in your listing.

**Highlight Your Best Reviews in the Description** – Guests scrolling through listings tend to skim details, so pulling a standout review or two into your listing's main description can grab their attention.

**Keep Your Listing Active & Updated** – Frequently updating your listing, adjusting pricing, and responding to guest inquiries quickly can help improve your ranking within TripAdvisor's search results.

## A TripAdvisor Host Story

A host in Byron Bay decided to list their beachfront rental on TripAdvisor, thinking it wouldn't make much of a difference. Within a few months, they noticed **a steady stream of bookings from international travelers**, particularly from Europe. Turns out, their property was appearing **at the top of Google searches for "best places to stay in Byron Bay"**—all because TripAdvisor's SEO game is that strong. Now, 50% of their bookings come from TripAdvisor, simply because their property ranks high in search results, thanks to **glowing reviews from past guests.**

## Final Thoughts: Should You Use These Platforms?

**If you want to diversify your bookings and reduce Airbnb dependence, YES.**

**If you're tired of Airbnb's constant changes and policies, YES.**

**If you want fewer party guests and more families or corporate travelers, YES.**

Each of these platforms has its **own strengths and audience**, and using them strategically can help fill your calendar, reduce risk, and boost profits. The beauty of these "underdog platforms" is that they allow you to **diversify your bookings** in a way that makes your business more resilient. By listing your property across multiple sites, you're opening the door to different types of guests—families on VRBO, business travelers on Expedia, and international vacationers on TripAdvisor.

It's important to remember that no single platform can serve all your needs. While Airbnb and Booking.com might bring in the majority of your bookings, these secondary platforms can fill the gaps and create a well-rounded, stable stream of income. Think of it like an investment portfolio—you wouldn't put all your money into one stock, so why rely on just one booking channel?

So, whether it's **VRBO for longer stays, Expedia for business travelers, or TripAdvisor for high-rated vacation rentals**, these platforms could be your secret weapon for **better, more stable bookings**. By optimizing your listings for their unique audiences, you're not only reaching more potential guests, but you're also ensuring that your short-term rental business remains profitable and adaptable no matter what changes come your way.

The key takeaway? **Diversify, optimize, and strategize.** At the end of the day, hosting success isn't about **crossing your fingers and hoping Airbnb's algorithm blesses you with bookings**. It's about **taking control**, **expanding your reach**, and **making sure your calendar stays full—on your terms.**

The more **booking platforms you master**, the more **resilient and profitable** your hosting journey will be. Think of it like **building an unstoppable rental empire**—one that doesn't crumble the second Airbnb changes its policies or Booking.com throws another curveball your way.

These platforms might not **steal the spotlight**, but they can **absolutely steal the show** when it comes to creating a thriving rental business. And let's be real—do you want to be the host who **sits around waiting for Airbnb to send them guests**, or do you want to be the host **actively filling their calendar with a well-rounded mix of travelers from multiple sources**?

Because here's the thing—**the best hosts don't just react; they strategize.** They **diversify their bookings like a stock market pro**,

**fine-tune their listings like a Michelin-star chef perfecting a recipe**, and **optimize their pricing like a travel hacker booking first-class flights for economy prices.**

So go forth and **list wisely**. Whether it's **VRBO's family-friendly travelers, Expedia's business-savvy guests, or TripAdvisor's international explorers**, the more platforms you tap into, the more **you future-proof your business.**

And if one platform suddenly decides to make life difficult? No problem—you've got **plenty of other income streams to keep you thriving.**

## Chapter Nine

# Building Resilience: Navigating Industry Challenges

The short-term rental industry can feel like you are on a treasure hunt—thrilling, lucrative, and, at times, so unpredictable that you wonder why you ever got on in the first place. One day, you're booked solid, raking in profits, and thinking about expanding. The next, a new regulation drops, the off-season hits, or a global event throws the entire travel industry into chaos, and suddenly, you're questioning every life choice that led you here. If you've been in this business long enough, you know that stability is an illusion, and the only way to survive is by being **adaptable, informed, and resilient.**

To make it in the short-term rental game, you have to be part entrepreneur, part problem-solver, part hospitality guru, and, on occasion, part therapist (because some guests will absolutely treat you like their personal concierge, handyman, and life coach all rolled into one). You're juggling everything from guest expectations to fluctuating market trends, all while trying to navigate the ever-changing maze of regulations that can make or break your business overnight.

This chapter dives deep into **how to stay ahead of industry challenges while keeping your sanity intact**. Whether it's understanding the latest legal hurdles, handling the dreaded off-season slowdown, or figuring out how to keep up with evolving guest preferences, this is your survival guide. By the end of this chapter, you'll be armed with practical strategies, insider tips, and a game plan for not just weathering the storm—but thriving in it.

## Dealing with Regulatory Changes and Compliance

Few things strike fear into the heart of a short-term rental host quite like the announcement of new short-term rental regulations. One moment, you're managing a thriving business, and the next, a sudden policy shift threatens to upend everything you've built. The landscape of short-term rentals is always evolving, and staying ahead of regulatory changes is not just about avoiding fines—it's about **future-proofing your business** and ensuring your rental empire stands the test of time.

Understanding the regulatory environment is more than just reading through dull municipal codes and legal jargon; it's about **safeguarding your investment and creating a sustainable business model**. Some hosts assume they can fly under the radar, only to get hit with a cease-and-desist letter or, worse, a hefty fine that wipes out months of profits. Others wait too long to adapt to new rules and find themselves scrambling at the last minute, trying to navigate confusing bureaucratic processes while still managing bookings.

The reality is that regulatory shifts can come out of nowhere. What was once a booming, unrestricted rental market can suddenly be subjected to strict zoning laws, occupancy limits, or even outright bans. But smart hosts know that **compliance isn't an obstacle—it's a strategy**. Those who take a proactive approach to staying informed and adjusting their business accordingly are the ones who continue to thrive while others struggle to catch up.

Staying compliant requires a **multi-pronged approach**. You need to:

- Keep an eye on city council meetings and legislative proposals.
- Build relationships with local policymakers to understand their stance on short-term rentals.
- Maintain all necessary permits and licenses well in advance to avoid disruptions.
- Have contingency plans in place, such as pivoting to mid-term rentals if short-term stays become restricted.

The best hosts aren't just **accommodators—they're strategists.** They recognize that regulations are part of the business landscape and use them as an opportunity to **strengthen their operations, not as a reason to panic**. Those who stay ahead of the curve aren't just compliant; they're resilient, prepared, and always one step ahead of the competition.

## Understanding Local Regulations: Know the Rules Before They Know You

The short-term rental industry can feel like a rollercoaster ride—thrilling, lucrative, and, at times, so unpredictable that you wonder why you ever got on in the first place. One day, you're booked solid, raking in profits, and thinking about expanding. The next, a new regulation drops, the off-season hits, or a global event throws the entire travel industry into chaos, and suddenly, you're questioning every life choice that led you here. If you've been in this business long enough, you know that stability is an illusion, and the only way to survive is by being **adaptable, informed, and resilient.**

To make it in the short-term rental game, you have to be part entrepreneur, part problem-solver, part hospitality guru, and, on occasion, part therapist (because some guests will absolutely treat you like their personal concierge, handyman, and life coach all rolled into one). You're juggling everything from guest expectations to fluctuating market trends, all while trying to navigate the ever-changing maze of regulations that can make or break your business overnight.

Lets do a deep dive into **how to stay ahead of industry challenges while keeping your sanity intact**. Whether it's understanding the latest legal hurdles, handling the dreaded off-season slowdown, or figuring out how to keep up with evolving guest preferences, this is your survival guide. By the end of this chapter, you'll be armed with practical strategies, insider tips, and a game plan for not just weathering the storm—but thriving in it.

- Local governments can be **unpredictable** when it comes to short-term rental laws. One year, they welcome STRs with open arms, and the next, they slap on restrictions faster than you can say "zoning ordinance."

- **Fines can be brutal.** In some cities, hosts face thousands of dollars in penalties for non-compliance. That's a lot of lost revenue.

- Even if you operate in a rental-friendly area, **ignorance isn't an excuse**. Just because you didn't know about a new rule doesn't mean the authorities will go easy on you.

## Keeping Updated with Changes: Stay Ahead of the Curve

You don't need to be a legal expert, but you do need to **keep an ear to the ground** when it comes to regulatory updates. Here's how:

- **Subscribe to local government newsletters** – Most cities publish updates on housing laws and zoning changes.

- **Join host networks and forums** – Fellow hosts are often the first to discuss upcoming regulation shifts. There's power in numbers!

- **Build a relationship with a local lawyer** – A 20-minute chat with an expert can save you thousands in compliance headaches.

- **Be proactive** – If you suspect that regulations are tightening, start looking at ways to adjust your business model (such as **pivoting to mid-term rentals** or exploring direct booking options).

## Permits & Regulations: The Not-So-Fun But Absolutely Necessary Side of Hosting

Look, I get it—**nobody** gets into the short-term rental game for the thrill of dealing with city hall and paperwork. But trust me, **handling permits and legal requirements upfront is one of the smartest things you can do for your business.** Nothing kills momentum faster than receiving a cease-and-desist letter just when bookings start rolling in.

Many hosts make the mistake of **diving headfirst into listing their property**, only to discover *after* they've got guests booked that they're missing a required permit, violating a zoning law, or—worst case—operating illegally. **By then, the damage is done, and the fines (or legal battles) can get expensive fast.** So, let's talk about how to **get ahead**

**of the red tape** and make sure your rental is legally compliant from day one.

## 1. Research Early: Don't Wait Until the Last Minute

One of the **biggest mistakes** new hosts make is assuming that **if their neighbor is renting on Airbnb, they can too.** Nope. Not every city, town, or neighborhood allows short-term rentals, and **even if they do, the rules can vary wildly.**

Before you even **take listing photos or set pricing**, do your homework:

Check your **city's short-term rental laws** – Some places ban them outright, while others have strict rules on how many nights per year you can rent.

See if you need a **business license** – Some cities require you to register your rental as a business, which may involve **fees and paperwork**.

Look at **zoning laws** – Even if short-term rentals are allowed in your city, your **specific neighborhood or building may have restrictions**.

Check **HOA rules** (if applicable) – Some **homeowner associations** have their own policies that may ban or restrict short-term rentals.

**Pro Tip:** If your city or county has a website, search for **"short-term rental regulations [your city]"** to get official guidelines. You can also call your local government office—**just prepare for some hold music.**

## 2. Understand Local Requirements: More Than Just a Permit

Even if short-term rentals are allowed where you live, **getting permission to operate isn't always as simple as filling out a form**. Some cities have **additional safety, insurance, and tax requirements** that you need to handle before hosting your first guest.

Here are some **common requirements** to look out for:

**Fire & Safety Inspections** – Some cities require an **official inspection** to ensure your rental meets fire safety standards. This might include:

- Smoke and carbon monoxide detectors in every room
- Fire extinguishers in key areas
- Clearly marked emergency exits
- Escape plans posted inside the unit

**Liability Insurance** – Some places **require proof of short-term rental insurance**, which is different from standard homeowner's insurance. Even if it's not mandatory, **having the right coverage protects you from lawsuits or damage claims.** Look for policies specifically designed for short-term rentals.

**Local Taxes & Fees** – Many cities require hosts to **collect and remit occupancy taxes** (sometimes called "hotel taxes" or "transient occupancy taxes"). Some platforms, like Airbnb and VRBO, **collect these automatically**, but **not always**—so double-check whether you need to **register and pay these yourself**.

**Guest Limits & Restrictions** – Some areas **cap the number of guests per rental**, require **minimum-night stays**, or **restrict the**

**number of bookings per year**. Make sure your rental setup aligns with local regulations.

**Pro Tip:** Many cities change their rules **frequently** (especially as short-term rentals grow in popularity), so check for updates **at least once a year**.

### 3. Keep Your Documentation Organized (Seriously, Don't Lose Anything)

The last thing you want is to be **scrambling for paperwork** when the city inspector shows up or when a permit renewal deadline sneaks up on you.

Create a **digital folder** (Google Drive, Dropbox, or whatever works for you) and keep copies of:

Your **rental permit/license**
Any required **safety inspection reports**
Your **short-term rental insurance policy**
Tax registration & receipts (if applicable)
Any **communications with local officials** about your rental

**Pro Tip:** Set calendar reminders for **permit renewals and tax deadlines** so you never get caught off guard. Some permits need to be renewed **annually**, while others last **several years**.

### 4. Follow Up Aggressively

If you think **applying for a permit means you'll get a quick response**, I've got some bad news. **Government agencies are notoriously slow**, and if you don't follow up, **your application could end up sitting in limbo indefinitely**.

Here's how to **speed things along**:

**Call and confirm receipt** of your application—don't assume it was processed just because you submitted it.

**Email follow-ups**—If a deadline passes and you still haven't heard back, check in.

**Show up in person if necessary**—Sometimes, face-to-face interaction **gets things moving faster than emails or phone calls.**

**Pro Tip:** When dealing with government employees, **be polite, but persistent**. Bureaucracy can be frustrating, but **being friendly and professional** can sometimes lead to **faster service and helpful guidance.**

## The Bottom Line: Yes, It's a Pain—But It's Worth It

Yes, this part of hosting is **tedious**. Yes, it's **frustrating**. But **getting the right permits and approvals upfront will save you an enormous amount of stress later**.

The alternative? **Fines, forced shutdowns, or even legal trouble.** And nothing ruins a hosting business faster than being told, "Oops, you can't rent here anymore."

Think of securing permits as **laying the foundation for a strong, legal, and profitable rental business**. Once you're compliant, you can focus on **what actually matters**—attracting bookings, creating amazing guest experiences, and making money without constantly looking over your shoulder.

Because, let's be honest—**the only thing worse than paperwork is losing your entire rental income over missing paperwork.** So take the time, do it right, and **host with confidence!**

**Implementing Compliance Strategies: Stay in the Clear**

Even if your area is currently relaxed about short-term rentals, that can change—and sometimes faster than you'd expect. Many cities have gone from fully embracing short-term rentals to slapping on restrictions seemingly overnight. Staying compliant isn't just about avoiding trouble—it's about safeguarding your investment and ensuring your business remains sustainable in the long run.

Being proactive about compliance means you're always **one step ahead of the game**. Instead of scrambling when new regulations pop up, you'll already have strategies in place to adapt. Keep detailed records, maintain proper licensing, and establish contingency plans like diversifying your rental strategies. Whether that means pivoting to mid-term stays, focusing on direct bookings, or even working with local policymakers to advocate for fair regulations, having a proactive mindset can mean the difference between thriving and scrambling to stay afloat.

Think of compliance as an ongoing process, not a one-time checklist. Laws and policies evolve, and so should your approach. The hosts who succeed in the long run are the ones who stay informed, adapt quickly, and treat compliance as an essential part of their business strategy—not just an annoying hurdle to jump over.

- **Create a compliance checklist** – Make sure you're meeting all local requirements.

- **Keep guests informed** – If your area has specific rules (like noise limits or parking restrictions), communicate them clearly.

- **Conduct regular audits** – Review your business practices every few months to make sure you're still on the right side of the law.

## Overcoming Seasonal Demand Fluctuations

Hosting would be a dream if demand were consistent year-round, but alas, **seasonal dips are real**. One month, you're turning guests away, juggling multiple inquiries, and feeling like a booking superstar. The next? You're staring at an empty calendar, refreshing your listings, and wondering if your property has suddenly developed an invisible force field keeping guests away.

This feast-or-famine cycle is one of the biggest challenges short-term rental hosts face, and it can wreak havoc on your revenue if you're not prepared. Learning to **ride the waves of demand** is key to maintaining steady income, keeping stress levels in check, and ensuring that your business remains sustainable no matter the season.

Rather than resigning yourself to slow periods, **smart hosts use this time to adapt and strategize**. Maybe it's an opportunity to attract a different type of guest, tweak your pricing model, or use creative marketing to boost off-season bookings. Some hosts pivot to mid-term stays, others offer unique seasonal packages, and the truly proactive ones start planting the seeds for next season's peak demand. The key is to **think ahead, adjust your approach, and never settle for an empty calendar**.

## Identifying Peak and Off-Peak Seasons: Plan Like a Pro

In the world of short-term rentals, knowing when demand will peak or plummet is like having a crystal ball. Guests' travel behaviors shift with the seasons, events, and even the weather, so mastering the art of predicting these trends can save you from the dreaded "empty calendar syndrome." Here's how to stay ahead:

- **Dive into Historical Booking Data**: If you've been hosting for a while, your past bookings hold the key to your future. Look at which months were fully booked, when inquiries dropped off, and how far in advance guests secured their stays. Did you see a rush before the holidays? A lull after New Year's? Trends don't just give you answers—they give you a strategy.

- **Keep Tabs on Local Events and Tourism Trends**: A sleepy winter town might transform into a bustling hotspot during ski season. Local festivals, food fairs, conventions, or even quirky events like "The Annual Garlic Festival" can turn your quiet property into prime real estate. Stay informed, and highlight these events in your listings to attract attendees.

- **Know When to Adjust Pricing**: Price gouging during a slow season is the equivalent of charging for bottled water in a rainstorm—your guests will go elsewhere. On the flip side, charging bargain-basement prices during peak times leaves money on the table. Recognizing the ebb and flow of demand lets you strike a balance and maximize revenue.

## Adjusting Pricing Strategies: Dynamic Pricing is Your Best Friend

If managing pricing makes you break out in a cold sweat, welcome to the club. Deciding how much to charge, when to raise rates, and when to drop them can feel like trying to predict the stock market. Luckily, dynamic pricing tools like **PriceLabs** are here to save the day—and your sanity.

### Why PriceLabs is a Game-Changer

Imagine having a personal pricing expert who works 24/7, crunching numbers and analyzing market trends to keep you competitive. That's what PriceLabs does. It's the ultimate tool for hands-off pricing that ensures you're charging just the right amount at all times. PriceLabs scans real-time market data, adjusts your rates based on demand, and even accounts for special events or last-minute availability. No more guessing. No more Googling "how much do I charge for Easter weekend?"

PriceLabs also helps you uncover trends you might not notice yourself. For example, if there's a surge in demand for mid-week stays during a local conference, PriceLabs will bump your prices accordingly, ensuring you're not undervaluing your property. On the flip side, it can detect slow periods and suggest competitive rates or discounts to fill your calendar.

### Seasonal Discounts and Bundled Experiences

When it comes to attracting guests during off-peak times, **incentives are your best friend**. A seasonal discount or an attractive bundled package can make your property stand out. For instance, you could offer:

- **Winter Ski Deals**: Include lift passes or discounts at a local rental shop.
- **Wine Lover Packages**: Highlight nearby vineyards and offer a complimentary bottle of wine upon check-in.
- **Spa & Relaxation Getaways**: Partner with local spas to offer discounted treatments for guests.

These little extras don't just add value—they create memorable guest experiences, which lead to glowing reviews and repeat bookings.

## Test, Adjust, and Refine

The beauty of using tools like PriceLabs is that it empowers you to test different pricing strategies without the headache. Did a weekend special bring in last-minute guests? Great, try it again. Did raising rates for a local event boost your revenue? Even better. Dynamic pricing tools give you the flexibility to experiment and adapt, ensuring you're always one step ahead of market trends.

In short, PriceLabs takes the stress out of pricing, helping you optimize revenue with minimal effort. Paired with strategic seasonal discounts and creative bundled packages, it's your secret weapon for ensuring your property stays booked—and profitable—year-round.

## Diversifying Marketing Efforts: Cast a Wider Net

When it comes to marketing your short-term rental, don't put all your eggs in one basket (or, in this case, all your bookings on one platform). Diversifying your marketing efforts is like casting a wide net—you'll catch more guests, fill those empty calendar slots, and sleep better at night knowing you're not overly dependent on any single website's algorithmic whims.

### Use Multiple Booking Platforms

Relying on just Airbnb is like trying to balance on a one-legged stool—risky and uncomfortable. If Airbnb is slow, why not let **VRBO, Expedia, or TripAdvisor** pick up the slack? Each platform caters to a different audience:

- **VRBO**: Families, groups, and longer stays. They love full homes with plenty of space.

- **Expedia**: Business travelers, event attendees, and international tourists who are more used to booking hotels but might stumble upon your listing.

- **TripAdvisor**: Tourists who want accommodations with great reviews and high credibility.

By listing your property across multiple platforms, you increase your visibility and reduce the risk of a quiet month turning into a financial drought. Plus, it's like playing the dating game with platforms—one of them is bound to be your match.

## Target Niche Markets

Not every traveler is the same. Some are digital nomads, others are pet parents, and some are just looking for a cozy spot to celebrate their honeymoon. Cater to these niche markets by tailoring your offerings:

- Add a **dedicated workspace** and high-speed Wi-Fi to attract the "working vacation" crowd.
- Make your rental **pet-friendly** by providing a comfy dog bed and some treats.
- Add small extras for specific groups, like board games for families, a romantic welcome basket for couples, or even a guide to the best gluten-free restaurants for health-conscious travelers.

By speaking directly to a specific audience, you'll attract guests who feel like your space was made just for them.

## Engage Past Guests

Your past guests are low-hanging fruit—they already know your property and (hopefully) loved their stay. Keep them coming back by:

- Offering **exclusive discounts** for repeat bookings.
- Sending personalized emails with phrases like, "We'd love to host you again!"

- Sharing insider updates, like a new hot tub installation or fun local events, to entice their return.

Loyalty is one of the easiest (and cheapest) ways to keep your calendar full, and repeat guests are far more likely to treat your property with care.

## Expanding Rental Offerings: Think Outside the Box

Sometimes, filling your calendar means thinking beyond the traditional weekend getaway. By expanding your rental offerings, you can attract new guests and make your property stand out in a crowded market.

### Offer Long-Term Stays During Slow Months

During the off-season, pivoting to **long-term stays** can stabilize your income. Digital nomads, relocating families, or even locals in need of temporary housing are all potential guests for month-long bookings. Plus, long-term stays mean fewer turnovers, less cleaning, and more time to relax.

Sweeten the deal by offering discounts for 30-day stays or including utilities, Wi-Fi, and a welcome basket. Predictable revenue + less work = happy host.

### Create Unique Experiences

A bed and a roof are fine, but an **experience** is what keeps guests talking (and reviewing). Create packages or themed stays to attract bookings:

- A **cozy winter package** with hot cocoa, blankets, and a roaring firepit.

- A **wine-lover's retreat** that includes tasting recommendations and a complimentary bottle.
- A **family fun deal** with board games, a popcorn machine, and a list of local kid-friendly activities.

These touches don't just fill your calendar—they turn your rental into a memory-making machine.

### Partner with Local Businesses

Team up with nearby restaurants, spas, or tour operators to offer exclusive perks

## Adapting to Changing Market Trends

If there's one constant in the rental industry, it's **change**—and it's relentless. What worked five years ago might be obsolete today, and what's trending now could be irrelevant tomorrow. From shifting guest expectations to ever-evolving booking platform policies, successful hosts don't just react to change—they anticipate and embrace it.

Staying flexible and adaptable ensures you remain **profitable and competitive**, but it also allows you to innovate ahead of the curve. Whether it's integrating new technology, adjusting to travel trends, or pivoting when market conditions shift, the ability to adapt separates the struggling hosts from the thriving ones.

Think about how the industry has evolved—self-check-ins, smart home technology, sustainability initiatives, and remote work-friendly rentals weren't top priorities a decade ago, but today they're practically essential. Hosts who saw these shifts early gained a major competitive edge, while those who resisted change found themselves scrambling to keep up.

The key is to always be **learning, testing, and refining**. The best hosts monitor guest behavior, experiment with new strategies, and aren't afraid to tweak their offerings. Standing still in this industry isn't an option—either you evolve, or you risk getting left behind.

## Staying Informed About Industry Trends: Knowledge is Power (and More Bookings!)

Running a successful short-term rental business isn't just about **setting up a great listing and hoping for the best**—it's about **staying ahead of the game, adapting to guest trends, and making sure your business evolves with the industry.** The world of hospitality is constantly changing, and **what worked last year might not be enough to keep you competitive today.**

Think of it this way: **Would you trust a restaurant that hasn't updated its menu since 2005?** Of course not. Guests expect **fresh, relevant, and modern experiences** when they travel, and staying informed about industry trends helps you **deliver exactly what they're looking for.**

## Keep Track of Emerging Guest Preferences (Because Tastes Change!)

Travelers **aren't looking for the same things they were five years ago**, and guest preferences shift based on everything from **technology to sustainability trends to economic changes.** If you're not adjusting your rental to meet **what today's guests want**, you could be **leaving money on the table.**

Here are some **guest preferences currently shaping the industry** (and why they matter to you):

**Eco-Friendly & Sustainable Stays** – More travelers **want to book accommodations that align with their values**—and **sustainability is at the top of the list.** Guests are actively looking for:

✔ Energy-efficient homes (LED lighting, solar power, smart thermostats).

✔ Recycling & composting options.

✔ Organic or locally sourced toiletries & cleaning products.

✔ Green certifications (like LEED or eco-labels for sustainable stays).

**How to Use This:** Even small changes—like switching to refillable soap dispensers or adding a **"green stay" feature** (offering guests the choice to skip daily cleaning to save water)—can appeal to **eco-conscious travelers** and set your listing apart.

**Smart Home Features** – Guests love **tech that makes their stay easier and more convenient**.

✔ Smart locks (easy check-in & security).

✔ Voice-controlled assistants (Alexa, Google Home).

✔ Wi-Fi-enabled thermostats (guests can adjust the temp without calling you).

✔ High-speed internet (especially crucial for remote workers).

**How to Use This: Highlight your smart home features in your listing!** If a guest has to **ask** whether your property has fast Wi-Fi, you've already lost the sale.

**The Rise of "Workation" & Remote Work Stays** – More professionals are **combining work & travel**, meaning they need spaces that **aren't just vacation homes but functional workspaces too**.

✔ Fast, reliable Wi-Fi.

✔ A dedicated workspace (a desk & ergonomic chair goes a long way).

✔ Extended-stay discounts.

✔ Quiet environments & good lighting for Zoom calls.

**How to Use This: Attract digital nomads and remote workers by optimizing your space for productivity**—and don't forget to add keywords like "remote work-friendly" in your listing title.

**Pet-Friendly Rentals Are in Demand** – More guests are **traveling with their furry friends**, and hotels often have **strict pet policies**—which means short-term rentals **can fill the gap**.

✔ Pet beds, bowls, and a few treats make a difference.

✔ Enclosed yards = major bonus.

✔ Pet fees? Absolutely. It's an easy upsell for travelers who need pet accommodations.

**How to Use This: If your property is pet-friendly, shout it from the rooftops.** Listings that **welcome pets often book faster & at higher rates.**

**Unique & Instagrammable Stays** – Travelers aren't just looking for a **place to sleep**—they want **an experience**. The rise of social media means guests are drawn to stays that are **visually appealing and unique**.

✔ Themed stays (cabin in the woods, desert escape, Scandinavian minimalist design).

✔ Instagrammable decor (stylish furniture, bold wallpaper, cozy reading nooks).

✔ Outdoor experiences (hammocks, fire pits, rooftop lounges).

**How to Use This: Make your space photogenic**—stylish touches, eye-catching decor, and unique design elements help your rental **stand out in a sea of generic listings.**

### 3. Attend Conferences & Stay Connected to the Industry

Sometimes, **the best way to learn is by hearing from the pros in person**. Whether it's a **conference, webinar, or industry event**, staying connected can give you insights **before trends become mainstream.**

**Top STR Conferences & Events to Consider Attending**

- **VRMA International Conference** (Biggest vacation rental event, great for networking).
- **STR Wealth Conference** (Focuses on profitability & high-level STR strategies).
- **The Book Direct Show** (Perfect if you're serious about direct bookings).
- **AirDNA Webinars** (Regular data-driven insights into the rental market).

If you can't attend in person, **many conferences offer virtual options or recorded sessions**—so there's no excuse for missing out.

## Final Thoughts: The Best Hosts Never Stop Learning

The **short-term rental industry is constantly evolving**, and what made **your listing successful last year might not be enough to keep you ahead today.** The best hosts **aren't just reacting to changes**—they're **predicting them, adapting early, and continuously improving their business.**

So make it a habit to:

**Read industry news & market reports** regularly.

**Join online communities** to learn from fellow hosts.

**Pay attention to guest trends** and adjust your offerings.

**Invest in professional development** (whether that's a conference, a course, or expert coaching).

Because in the world of short-term rentals, **knowledge isn't just power—it's profit.** The more **you know, the better you can adapt, and the more bookings (and higher earnings) you'll secure.**

## Embracing Technological Advancements: Work Smarter, Not Harder

Let's be honest—**running a short-term rental can feel like juggling flaming torches while riding a unicycle**. Between guest communications, bookings, turnovers, and maintenance, it's easy to get overwhelmed. But here's the good news: **you don't have to do everything**

**manually.** Thanks to technology, **you can automate the repetitive stuff**, make life easier for yourself, and create a **seamless experience for guests**. Here's how:

**Use Property Management Software (PMS)** – Think of this as your **virtual personal assistant**, handling **reservations, messaging, pricing adjustments, and calendar syncing across platforms**. Some great options? Hospitable, Guesty, and Lodgify. Instead of logging into five different booking sites every day, let the software do the work for you. (*Because your time is better spent sipping coffee, not updating calendars manually.*)

**Offer Self-Check-In with Smart Locks** – The days of **hiding keys under doormats** or **meeting guests at weird hours** are over. With a smart lock, guests can check in anytime with a unique code. Bonus? No more "I'm locked out" calls at 2 AM.

**Provide Virtual Tours** – In a sea of listings, **how do you stand out?** By giving guests **a virtual walkthrough of your space** before they even book. Not only does this **boost your listing's appeal**, but it also helps guests know exactly what to expect—**meaning fewer complaints and higher satisfaction.**

**Automate Guest Messaging** – Platforms like Hospitable allow you to **schedule friendly reminders, check-in instructions, and follow-up messages** without lifting a finger. (*Your guests will think you're incredibly attentive, but really, it's just your tech game on point.*)

**Use Smart Home Tech** – Wi-Fi thermostats, voice assistants, and energy-efficient lighting not only **improve guest experience** but can **save you money** on utilities. Plus, who doesn't love the feeling of controlling the lights with their voice like some kind of futuristic overlord?

## Conducting Regular Competitor Analysis: Stay Ahead of the Game

If you think your listing is **the best on the block**, let me ask you this: **When was the last time you checked out your competition?**

The short-term rental market **is constantly evolving**, and what worked six months ago **might not cut it today**. The best hosts aren't just *reacting* to changes—they're **actively analyzing what's working and staying ahead of the curve.**

**See What Similar Listings Are Doing** – Your competitors aren't just random people renting out their spaces—they're **real-time market research opportunities.** Check their:

✔ **Pricing** – Are they charging more or less than you? Are they adjusting rates seasonally?

✔ **Amenities** – Are they offering something you're not? (Free breakfast? Bikes? A dedicated workspace?)

✔ **Guest Reviews** – What are **their** guests loving or complaining about? (Pro tip: If guests keep raving about someone's **super comfy mattress**, it might be time for an upgrade.)

**Adjust Your Strategy Accordingly** – Found out your competitors are offering **free parking, welcome gifts, or personalized local guides**? Maybe it's time to **level up your own offering**. And if you spot weaknesses in their service, capitalize on them. (*"Oh, they don't provide AC in summer? Time to highlight my climate-controlled paradise!"*)

## Iterating Your Service Offerings: Evolve or Get Left Behind

The best hosts don't just **list their property and hope for the best**—they **adapt, refine, and constantly improve** based on guest feedback and market trends. In other words, **you either evolve, or you become the Blockbuster of short-term rentals.**

**Act on Guest Feedback** – If three different guests mention that the **Wi-Fi signal is weak in the bedroom**, guess what? It's time for a Wi-Fi extender. If multiple people suggest **blackout curtains** because the sun turns your bedroom into a nuclear explosion at 6 AM, listen to them. (*Happy guests = repeat guests = better reviews = more bookings.*)

**Experiment with New Amenities** – The right amenities can **make or break** a booking decision. Try:

✔ **Fast Wi-Fi & Workspaces** – Remote workers are traveling more than ever. Adding **a desk, a comfy chair, and extra outlets** can instantly attract digital nomads.

✔ **Hot Tubs for Winter Travelers** – Because nothing says *luxury* like soaking in **steamy, bubbly goodness under the stars.**

✔ **Pet-Friendly Features** – More guests are bringing their furry friends. Adding **a dog bed, food bowls, or a fenced yard** could open your listing to an entirely **new market**.

**Target New Demographics** – If your usual guests are **couples on weekend getaways**, why not open up to **solo travelers, digital nomads, or families**? Small changes like **single-guest discounts, kid-friendly features, or extended stay options** can bring in **new types of bookings.**

**Pro Tip:** Not sure what new features or perks to add? **Test them for a month.** See if it moves the needle. If bookings increase, keep it. If not, pivot to something else.

## Conclusion: Stay Resilient, Stay Profitable

The short-term rental industry is not for the faint of heart, but with the right strategies, you can **thrive despite the challenges**. Whether it's navigating legal hurdles, keeping bookings steady year-round, or staying ahead of market trends, resilience is **the secret sauce to long-term success**. By staying informed, adapting quickly, and implementing smart strategies, you'll not only **survive** industry challenges—you'll master them.

Success in this business isn't about avoiding obstacles—it's about knowing how to tackle them head-on. Regulatory shifts? You've got compliance strategies in place. Seasonal slumps? You've diversified your marketing and pricing. Changing guest preferences? You're keeping up with the trends and offering exactly what they want.

The best hosts are those who embrace the **ever-changing landscape** of short-term rentals with creativity and confidence. Instead of fearing change, see it as an opportunity to refine your business, expand your reach, and optimize your listings. A sudden market shift doesn't mean disaster—it just means it's time to pivot, innovate, and stay ahead of the competition.

The most successful hosts aren't necessarily the ones with the most properties or the fanciest interiors—they're the ones who **think ahead, plan for disruptions, and continuously evolve**. They build a brand that stands out, provide unforgettable guest experiences, and create a business model that can withstand economic ups and downs.

So keep learning, stay flexible, and **lean into the challenges** that come your way. The rental market will always change, but with the right mindset and strategies, you'll be the host who not only weathers the storm but **thrives in any environment**.

# Chapter Ten

# Case Studies and Success Stories – Stories From Some Of The Best

Grab a coffee and settle in. The short-term rental world is overflowing with stories of hosts who have unlocked the secrets to success through **direct bookings, innovative marketing, and smart diversification**. These hosts are proof that with the right strategies, anyone can thrive in this dynamic industry. Their lessons aren't just valuable—they're transformational. Why struggle through the same challenges when you can learn from the best and fast-track your way to success?

Imagine being a host who no longer relies solely on Airbnb's shifting algorithms or absorbs the painful 15-20% commission fees from booking platforms. Picture yourself running a rental business that is resilient, profitable, and totally in your control. That's what the hosts in this chapter have achieved, and now, you can too.

This chapter is your backstage pass to real-world success stories. You'll meet the hosts who took control of their destiny, abandoned the status quo, and created thriving short-term rental empires. Some of them mastered the art of direct bookings and turned their websites into guest magnets. Others crafted marketing campaigns so clever they'd make a Fortune 500 marketer jealous. And a few diversified so brilliantly they became bulletproof against economic ups and downs.

What's more, these stories don't just highlight their successes—they reveal their strategies, mistakes, and the lessons they learned along the way. You'll gain actionable insights that you can implement immediately, whether you're just starting out or looking to take your rental business to new heights.

Get ready to be inspired by the hosts who stopped playing by everyone else's rules and built their businesses on their own terms. Their journeys aren't just motivational; they're a roadmap for your own success. If you're ready to take your short-term rental game to the next level, let's dive in.

## Analyzing Successful Direct Booking Strategies: How Hosts Took Control & Won

Sure, Airbnb and other platforms are fantastic for visibility—they're basically the rock stars of the short-term rental world, with millions of travelers scrolling through their listings daily. But let's get real for a moment: **paying 15-20% in fees? Ouch.** That's like hosting a party where Airbnb eats half the cake you baked. It's painful, especially when you think about all the time, effort, and expense you put into creating a top-tier guest experience.

These hosts, however, weren't about to let platform fees bleed their profits dry. Instead, they rolled up their sleeves, sharpened their pencils (or, let's be honest, opened their laptops), and built **direct booking pipelines** so enticing that guests couldn't resist. It wasn't just about saving money; it was about **taking back control** of their business and forging meaningful connections with their guests.

By ditching the middleman—or at least reducing their dependence on him—they stopped playing by platform algorithms and started playing their own game. Their secret weapons? Sleek websites, irresistible incentives, and an unshakable commitment to wowing their guests. Now, they're not just hosts—they're brand builders, loyalty creators, and profit protectors. Oh, and they're laughing all the way to the bank, without losing a chunk of their earnings along the way.

## Case Study: The Family Cottage – Turning a Website into a Booking Magnet

Meet the Johnsons, a family who turned their charming lakeside cottage into a direct booking powerhouse. Instead of relying on platforms, they revamped their website to make the booking process **as smooth as butter** (because nobody likes a clunky checkout experience).

### What Worked:

- **Streamlined Website UX**: Guests could book in **three clicks**—no frustrating back-and-forth emails, just instant confirmations.
- **Incentives for Direct Bookings**: They offered a **5% discount + a welcome gift** for guests who booked directly, which made travelers feel special *and* saved them money.
- **Clear Communication on Direct Benefits**: Instead of just saying, *"Book direct to save money!"*, they explained why: **lower prices, better customer service, and early check-in perks**.

*Lesson:* **The easier and more rewarding you make direct booking, the more guests will choose it.**

### Extra Tip:

The Johnsons also started **collecting guest emails** and sending out **seasonal offers**, ensuring past visitors had a reason to return.

## Case Study: Urban Loft Experience – The Power of Referral Marketing

Jake owns a stylish urban loft, and instead of throwing money at ads, he let his guests **do the marketing for him.** His secret? **A tailored referral program** that turned satisfied guests into booking machines.

### What Worked:

- **Referral Discounts**: Guests who referred a friend got **$50 off their next stay**, and their friend got **a 10% discount**—a win-win for everyone.
- **Personalized Follow-Ups**: He didn't just send generic thank-you emails. He followed up with **custom messages and an easy referral link** guests could share.
- **Guest Engagement Surveys**: Feedback wasn't just collected—it was **used** to improve the experience and **increase loyalty.**

*Lesson:* **Give guests a reason to talk about your rental, and they'll send new business your way.**

### Extra Tip:

Jake also included a **VIP loyalty program** where guests who referred multiple friends unlocked **early check-ins and free upgrades**.

## Case Study: Country Bungalow – Community Ties That Drove Bookings

Mary's charming countryside bungalow wasn't just a place to stay—it was an **experience**. She **partnered with local businesses** and hosted **seasonal events** to create a rental that was always buzzing with activity.

### What Worked:

- **Seasonal Community Events**: Think **fall harvest weekends, summer wine tastings, and winter bonfires**—guests loved the exclusivity.
- **Local Business Collabs**: Partnering with a **nearby bakery for breakfast packages** and **a local farm for horseback rides** added extra value.
- **Word-of-Mouth Magic**: Local business owners sent her **tons of referrals**, turning the bungalow into a local **must-stay spot.**

*Lesson:* **If your rental feels like part of the community, guests (and locals) will rave about it.**

### Extra Tip:

Mary also leveraged **local Facebook groups** to share upcoming events and showcase her rental as a top spot for visitors.

## Examining Innovative Marketing Campaigns: Hosts Who Got Creative & Won Big

Sometimes, simply throwing up a listing and hoping for the best isn't enough. In a world where **competition is fierce and algorithms change overnight**, the best hosts know that success isn't about luck—it's about strategy.

If you want to **keep your calendar full**, you can't just sit back and wait for guests to find you. You need to **make your property irresistible**, create a buzz, and give people a reason to choose *your* rental over the hundreds of others available. The most successful hosts aren't just property owners—they're storytellers, brand builders, and marketing wizards who know how to make an impression.

These hosts didn't just rely on a single listing platform; they took control of their visibility. They leveraged social media, built referral programs, and created **niche marketing strategies** that spoke directly to their ideal guests. Some mastered the art of **seasonal promotions**, while others turned their properties into an experience guests couldn't wait to book. Whether it was collaborating with influencers, crafting viral content, or engaging with local businesses to boost their presence, they all understood one thing: **visibility leads to bookings, and bookings lead to profit.**

The result? More direct bookings, loyal repeat guests, and a business that doesn't crumble under algorithm changes or off-season slumps. These marketing masterminds didn't just get noticed—they got booked. Let's dive into their strategies and uncover the **marketing magic** that made all the difference.

### Campaign: Social Media Influencer Partnerships

Lisa had a beach villa that was beautiful but buried under **thousands** of similar listings. Her solution? **Influencer marketing.**

### What Worked:

- **Teaming Up with Local Travel Influencers**: Instead of paying for ads, she let influencers **stay for free in exchange for exposure.**
- **Gorgeous, Shareable Content**: The influencers created **stunning Instagram Reels & TikToks** that made her villa look like a dream.
- **Consistent Referrals**: After the campaign, guests kept booking *because they had seen it on social media!*

*Lesson:* **Social proof works—people trust recommendations from people they follow more than ads.**

### Campaign: Referral Contests – Making Guests Your Marketers

Instead of waiting for referrals to happen, Sam *made* them happen—with a **guest referral contest.**

### What Worked:

- Guests who referred the most friends got a **free weekend stay.**
- Every referral entered them into a **monthly giveaway for fun prizes.**
- **Guests got competitive**—some people referred 5-10 friends just for a chance to win!

*Lesson:* **People love a good competition—turn referrals into a game, and guests will market your rental for you.**

### Extra Tip:

Sam also followed up with referred guests, offering them a **"first-time guest bonus"** to increase conversion rates.

## Final Takeaways: Lessons from the Pros

Success in short-term rentals isn't just about listing a property and waiting for bookings to roll in—it's about **taking charge, thinking strategically, and continuously evolving**. The hosts featured in this chapter didn't sit back and hope for the best; they made deliberate moves to build a profitable, sustainable business. Whether it was leveraging direct bookings, crafting brilliant marketing campaigns, or diversifying their revenue streams, they took control of their success—and so can you.

If there's one lesson that stands out from these case studies, it's this: **opportunity doesn't knock—it's built.** The best hosts are always looking ahead, anticipating shifts in the market, and adapting their strategies. They don't just react to change; they embrace it, using every challenge as an opportunity to improve. From refining their direct booking systems to building community relationships and using smart marketing tactics, they've proven that there's always a way to grow and thrive.

But let's be honest—running a short-term rental business isn't always smooth sailing. There will be slow seasons, difficult guests, and unexpected hurdles. The difference between hosts who struggle and those who succeed is **resilience, creativity, and a willingness to experiment**. Every setback is a lesson, every challenge is a chance to improve, and every success is a stepping stone to even greater achievements.

The strategies and success stories shared here are not just inspiration; they're **a roadmap for your own journey**. Take what resonates, apply it to your business, and watch how small tweaks and innovative ideas can lead to incredible results. The next great case study in short-term rentals could be yours. If these case studies prove anything, it's that **thinking outside the box works**. Whether it's optimizing for direct bookings, running smart marketing campaigns, or diversifying your offerings, the best hosts are the ones who **take control and innovate**.

## Action Steps for You: Because More Direct Bookings = More Money

So, you're serious about leveling up your direct booking game? **Good.** Because relying solely on Airbnb and other platforms is like having a job where your boss can randomly cut your pay, change the rules, or just fire you overnight. **Direct bookings put YOU in control**—of your income, your guest relationships, and your business growth.

But the key to **getting more direct bookings isn't just having a "Book Now" button on your website and hoping for the best**. You need to **actively drive traffic, build trust, and make it so easy (and rewarding) for guests to book directly that they never even consider using a third-party site.**

Here's what you need to do:

## 1. Assess Your Current Direct Booking Strategy (Be Brutally Honest!)

Ask yourself: **Is my direct booking process easy, rewarding, and transparent? Or is it a confusing mess that makes guests run back to Airbnb?**

**Do I have a professional-looking website?** If your site looks like it was made in 2005 and requires guests to "email for availability," **that's a problem.** You need an easy-to-navigate, modern website with instant booking capabilities.

**Is my booking process ridiculously simple?** Guests should be able to book in **3 clicks or less**. If they have to jump through multiple forms, verify their identity like they're applying for a passport, or wait for a response, **you're losing them**.

**Are guests getting a reason to book directly?** What's in it for them? Consider offering:

- **Discounted rates for direct bookings** (since you're not paying platform fees, pass some of those savings on).
- **Exclusive perks** (early check-in, late check-out, a free bottle of wine, or local goodies).
- **More flexible cancellation policies** (without being reckless).

**Pro Tip:** Try **booking your own rental through your website** as if you were a guest. If anything feels clunky, confusing, or slow, **fix it.**

## 2. Consider a Referral Program (AKA, Get Your Guests to Do Your Marketing for You)

**Your past guests are GOLD.** If they had a great experience, they're likely to **recommend your place to friends and family**—but you need to **give them a nudge** to do it.

**Offer guests a discount or bonus for referring new bookings**

- Example: "Refer a friend, and they get 10% off their first stay. If they book, you get 10% off your next visit."
- This **incentivizes repeat stays** while encouraging new direct bookings.

**Give guests an easy way to refer people**

- Create a simple **referral link or promo code** they can share.

- Add a **"Share Your Stay"** card in your welcome binder with a QR code leading to your direct booking page.

**Encourage social sharing**

- Ask guests to tag your rental's Instagram or Facebook page in their posts (**bonus if they share your booking link**).
- Run a monthly giveaway: "Post a photo of your stay and tag us for a chance to win a free night!"

**Pro Tip:** People **trust personal recommendations** way more than ads. **Make it rewarding for guests to talk about you, and you'll get bookings without lifting a finger.**

## 3. Think About Community Partnerships (Because Your Town Is Full of Hidden Booking Opportunities)

If you want **more direct bookings**, start thinking beyond your usual guest sources. **Your local community can be a goldmine for steady bookings**—especially if you create win-win partnerships.

**Collaborate with local businesses**

- Partner with **wedding venues** (out-of-town guests need places to stay!).
- Connect with **event organizers** (marathons, festivals, business conferences).
- Team up with **local tour companies** (offer a stay + experience package).

**Target corporate travelers & relocation guests**

- Reach out to **HR departments at major companies in your area**. Offer **extended stay options** for relocating employees.
- List your property on **corporate housing sites like Furnished Finder** for mid-term stays.

**Work with real estate agents**

- New homeowners often need **short-term housing** while waiting to close on a property. Build a relationship with real estate agents so they send their clients your way.

**Pro Tip:** Local partnerships = **repeat business, longer stays, and fewer gaps in your calendar**. Don't just wait for travelers—**go where the bookings are and get in front of new audiences.**

## 4. Explore Social Media (Yes, Even If You Think You're "Not a Social Media Person")

Look, I get it. **Not everyone loves social media.** But when it comes to marketing your rental, **a strong social presence = more eyeballs on your listing = more direct bookings.**

**Create an Instagram page for your rental**

- Share **stunning photos, guest experiences, and local attractions**.
- Use hashtags like **#vacationrentals #airbnbsuperhost #yourcitygetaway** to get discovered.

- Post **behind-the-scenes content** (setting up for guests, cool decor updates, local events).

**Leverage Facebook Groups & Marketplace**

- Join **local travel, relocation, and short-term rental groups** where people actively look for stays.
- Post about last-minute availability and special offers.

**Run a simple influencer campaign**

- No, you don't need to pay **big influencers**—micro-influencers (**5k-50k followers**) in your area can be just as effective.
- Offer **a free night or a discount in exchange for a feature on their page**.
- A well-placed Instagram story can bring in **a flood of new bookings.**

**Pro Tip:** Social media isn't about **posting every day**—it's about **showing up consistently** and making your rental easy to find **when someone is searching for a stay in your area.**

At the end of the day, success in short-term rentals **isn't just about having a great property**—because there are plenty of beautiful homes out there that sit empty while their owners wonder why no one's booking. **It's about marketing, branding, and making smart business moves that keep your calendar full and your bank account happy.** If you take one thing away from this, let it be this: **don't put all your bookings in one basket (especially an Airbnb-branded one).** Diversifying your income streams isn't just a strategy—it's the difference between **thriving and stressing.** Crossing your fingers and hoping Airbnb's algorithm puts you on page one is not a business plan—it's wishful thinking. Instead, **stack the deck in your favor** by pulling in bookings from multiple sources—direct bookings, VRBO, Expedia, local partnerships, social media, and every other creative avenue you can think of. When you **control where your bookings come from, you control your business.** So keep learning, keep experimenting, and keep growing. **Because pretty soon, you'll be the host that others look at and think, "Damn, how are they doing it?"** And you'll just smile, sip your coffee (or wine), and know it's because you built something **smart, resilient, and completely in your control.**

## Chapter Eleven

# Future Trends in Short-Term Rentals – What's Next?

The short-term rental industry is evolving **faster than a guest who says they'll check out at 10 AM but is still sipping coffee at noon**—and trust me, we've all had that guest. What worked five years ago might not work today, and what's trending now could be as outdated as shag carpet by next season. But don't panic—this chapter is your **crystal ball into the future of short-term rentals** (minus the mystical fog and dramatic fortune-teller music). To stay ahead, hosts need to **anticipate changes, embrace new trends, and adapt**

**to shifting guest expectations**—or risk being left behind, wondering why their beautifully decorated rental is sitting empty. The good news? The future is filled with **exciting opportunities** for those who are willing to **think ahead, innovate, and roll with the punches** (or at least with the algorithm updates). From **eco-friendly stays** that cater to sustainability-conscious travelers, to **AI-powered guest experiences** that make life easier for both hosts and visitors, the next era of short-term rentals is shaping up to be dynamic, high-tech, and full of possibilities. And the best part? If you play your cards right, these trends can **work for you, boost your bookings, and keep your business thriving**. So grab a coffee (or a mimosa, we don't judge) and let's dive into the future of hosting!

## The Rise of Eco-Friendly and Sustainable Rentals

### Why Sustainability is More Than Just a Trend

Sustainability isn't just a buzzword—it's becoming a **major factor in travel decisions**. More guests than ever are seeking out rentals that prioritize eco-friendly practices. And no, we're not just talking about putting a recycling bin in the corner and calling it a day. Travelers want properties that genuinely **reduce environmental impact**, from energy efficiency to responsible waste management.

A 2023 survey found that over **80% of travelers prefer to stay in sustainable accommodations**. That means hosts who prioritize green practices aren't just helping the planet—they're **attracting more guests**

**and increasing their revenue**. Sustainability isn't a **nice-to-have** anymore; it's a **business strategy** that gives you a competitive edge.

## How to Make Your Rental More Eco-Friendly

- **Upgrade to Energy-Efficient Appliances** – Swap out those ancient, energy-guzzling appliances for ENERGY STAR-rated options.
- **Install Smart Thermostats** – Guests may not think to adjust the temperature, but your smart thermostat will.
- **Use LED Lighting** – It lasts longer, uses less power, and makes your electric bill look a little less terrifying.
- **Provide Refillable Toiletries** – Say goodbye to single-use plastic bottles.
- **Reduce Waste with Recycling and Composting** – Make it easy for guests by clearly labeling bins.
- **Offer Incentives for Sustainable Travel** – Discount stays for guests who arrive via public transport or bike instead of driving.

## Marketing Your Green Rental

If you've invested in sustainability, **make sure guests know about it!**

- Highlight your eco-friendly initiatives in your listing description.

- Use social media to showcase your green upgrades (Instagram loves a good solar panel photo).
- Partner with eco-tourism businesses to attract **environmentally conscious travelers**.

Sustainability isn't just good for the environment—it's **great for business**. And with the rise of **eco-tourism**, properties that align with these values will only continue to thrive.

## Technological Advancements in Guest Management

If you've ever spent an hour coordinating check-in details with a guest who *still* doesn't understand how to use a keypad, you'll appreciate how much technology is transforming the rental space. The days of manual processes and **constantly texting guests directions** are fading. Instead, we're entering an era where **automation, smart home tech, and AI-driven services** are making hosting easier, smoother, and frankly, way less stressful.

### The Smart Home Revolution

From voice-activated assistants to self-adjusting climate control, guests are expecting a **seamless, tech-enabled experience**. Smart home integration isn't just a convenience—it's becoming a **must-have** for modern rentals.

#### Must-Have Smart Tech for Hosts:

- **Smart Locks** – No more lost keys or last-minute lockouts.
- **Smart Thermostats** – Keeps energy use low while keeping guests comfortable.
- **Voice-Controlled Assistants (Alexa, Google Home)** – Guests love asking, *"Alexa, where's the best pizza in town?"*
- **Automated Lighting** – Because guests *will* forget to turn off the lights.
- **Noise Monitoring Devices** – Alert you before your rental turns into a nightclub.

## Guest Management Software – Your Virtual Assistant

If you've ever spent an hour coordinating check-in details with a guest who *still* doesn't understand how to use a keypad, you'll appreciate how much technology is transforming the rental space. The days of manual processes and **constantly texting guests directions** are fading—finally! Instead, we're entering an era where **automation, smart home tech, and AI-driven services** are making hosting easier, smoother, and frankly, way less stressful.

One of the biggest game-changers? **BetsyAI**—a powerhouse tool I personally use and absolutely love. BetsyAI is like having an ultra-efficient co-host that never sleeps, never forgets details, and never gets frustrated answering the same guest questions over and over again. It automates guest communication, provides instant responses, and even customizes replies based on guest preferences and previous interactions. Basically, it's like cloning yourself, but without the added expense of a second mortgage.

Imagine a world where you're not explaining to a grown adult how to enter a four-digit code correctly. A world where you're not triple-confirming check-in details at 1 AM because a guest just "didn't see the email." That world is now. **Smart locks** let guests in without hassle, **automated messages** remind them where to find things before they even ask, and **AI-driven assistants like BetsyAI** are standing by to answer the "What's the Wi-Fi password?" question before it even leaves their lips.

And it's not just about convenience—it's about **efficiency and guest satisfaction**. The less time you spend troubleshooting minor issues, the more time you have to focus on growing your business, refining your guest experience, or, you know, actually relaxing (because let's be real, you deserve it).

Welcome to the future of hosting, where technology isn't just a fancy add-on—it's your new best friend, and BetsyAI is the sidekick you didn't know you needed.

Imagine a world where you're not explaining to a grown adult how to enter a four-digit code correctly. A world where you're not triple-confirming check-in details at 1 AM because a guest just "didn't see the email." That world is now. Smart locks let guests in without hassle, automated messages remind them where to find things before they even ask, and AI-driven assistants are standing by to answer the "What's the Wi-Fi password?" question before it even leaves their lips.

And it's not just about convenience—it's about **efficiency and guest satisfaction**. The less time you spend troubleshooting minor issues, the more time you have to focus on growing your business, refining your guest experience, or, you know, actually relaxing.

Welcome to the future of hosting, where technology isn't just a fancy add-on—it's your new best friend.

### Top Benefits of Guest Management Software:

- **Automates Guest Communication** – Instant responses and scheduled messages = happy guests.
- **Syncs Your Calendar** – Prevents double bookings across platforms.
- **Streamlines Check-In and Check-Out** – No more midnight phone calls about where the keys are.

### The Future of Guest Tech: What's Coming Next?

- **AI-Powered Chatbots** – Imagine a bot answering guest questions instantly, even at 2 AM.
- **Facial Recognition Check-In** – Airbnb already experimented with it—soon, guests may just need their face to unlock your rental.
- **Blockchain-Based Transactions** – The future of secure pay-

ments? Maybe!

Tech isn't replacing hosts—it's **freeing them up** to focus on what really matters: **creating incredible guest experiences**.

## Predicting Future Shifts in Guest Preferences

Guest expectations are constantly evolving, and what travelers want today **may not be what they want tomorrow**—because let's face it, trends move faster than a guest who suddenly remembers checkout was an hour ago. One day, everyone wants minimalist Scandinavian-style Airbnbs, and the next, they're hunting for jungle treehouses with outdoor showers. The key to long-term success? **Adaptability, foresight, and a little bit of host intuition.** Understanding these shifts now will help you **stay ahead of the curve** and ensure your rental remains booked, profitable, and appealing to guests who are always looking for the next best thing. Whether it's integrating tech for digital nomads, creating Instagrammable spaces, or offering local experiences that turn a simple stay into a memory-making adventure, the hosts who embrace change rather than fear it will continue to thrive. The reality is, travelers today want **more than just a place to sleep**—they want connection, experiences, and something worth bragging about on social media. Keeping up with these shifts isn't just a survival tactic; it's an opportunity to **position your rental as a forward-thinking, guest-centric haven.** So, if your last major update was swapping out DVDs for a Netflix login, it might be time to start thinking bigger!

## 1. The Rise of "Workations" and Remote Work Stays

Remote work has **changed the game**. More professionals are opting for **longer stays in inspiring locations**, turning rentals into **temporary offices, creative studios, and even makeshift yoga retreats**. The lines between work and travel have blurred, and digital nomads, freelancers, and corporate professionals alike are seizing the opportunity to swap dreary cubicles for scenic workspaces.

If your space isn't optimized for remote workers, you could be missing out on a **massive, high-value market**. These guests aren't just booking for a weekend getaway; they're booking for **weeks or even months at a time**, providing steady income and fewer turnovers. Plus, they tend to treat your space with more care—because no one wants to work on a broken chair or deal with unreliable Wi-Fi when they have deadlines looming.

To make your property remote-worker friendly, start with the essentials:

- **Offer Fast & Reliable Wi-Fi** – No one wants a video call that freezes mid-sentence, making them look like a glitchy robot.

- **Set Up a Dedicated Work Area** – A desk, ergonomic chair, and good lighting go a long way. Bonus points for a fancy coffee machine nearby.

- **Provide Long-Stay Discounts** – A lower nightly rate for 30-day stays can **fill your calendar faster** while still keeping revenue high.

- **Stock Up on Office Essentials** – A few extras like a printer, ring light, or noise-canceling headphones can set you apart from the competition.

- **Market Your Space as a Workation Destination** – Highlight nearby coffee shops, coworking spaces, and fast-food places that will deliver when work gets intense.

With the rise of **hybrid work models** and **work-from-anywhere policies**, the demand for **remote-friendly rentals** isn't slowing down anytime soon. The hosts who adapt to this trend will enjoy higher occupancy rates, longer bookings, and, let's be honest—probably fewer wild party guests.

## 2. Experience-Based Travel is Booming

Today's guests aren't just looking for a place to sleep—they want **memorable, immersive experiences that they can brag about to their friends, post on social media, and remember long after their stay is over**. Gone are the days when a comfy bed and free Wi-Fi were enough to impress. Now, guests are looking for that "wow" factor—whether it's waking up in a treehouse, sipping wine under fairy lights in a secret garden, or soaking in a clawfoot tub with a breathtaking mountain view.

Modern travelers want experiences that make them **feel something**—adventure, relaxation, exclusivity, or a sense of belonging. They want **local flavor**, not just a cookie-cutter hotel experience in disguise. They're on the hunt for places that offer more than just accommodation—whether it's a farm stay where they can feed baby goats, a lakeside cabin with a private chef experience, or an urban loft that comes with an itinerary of hidden city gems curated by the host.

And let's not forget social media's role in all of this. If a rental isn't "Instagrammable," is it even worth booking? Guests today love accommodations that come with built-in photo ops—think neon signs with catchy phrases, unique art pieces, or rooftop hammocks with unbeatable views. The more photogenic, the better!

As a host, this shift in guest expectations is an opportunity to get creative. How can you make your rental stand out? What little extras can you provide that turn a standard stay into an unforgettable experience? Because when you create a space that's **more than just a place to sleep**, you're not just attracting guests—you're creating lifelong fans who will rave about their stay and come back for more.

### How to Tap into This Trend:

- **Offer Local Experiences** – Think cooking classes, guided hikes, or surf lessons.
- **Showcase Unique Features** – Treehouse rental? Private vineyard? Make it stand out.
- **Personalize Stays** – Small touches, like handwritten notes and curated local recommendations, go a long way.

### 3. The Demand for Unique & Instagrammable Rentals

Social media has **completely changed how people choose accommodations**. It's not just about comfort and location anymore—it's about **aesthetic, vibe, and that all-important Instagram moment**. Because let's face it, if a trip isn't documented with a dreamy balcony coffee shot, did it even happen?

Travelers today suffer from **serious FOMO** (fear of missing out), and they want to stay in places that make their friends jealous. A cozy, stylish, or quirky rental isn't just a place to sleep—it's part of their travel experience, their content, their personal brand. If your property looks like it belongs in a home decor magazine, congratulations! You've just made someone's **"Dream Airbnb Stay" Pinterest board.** If it looks like a generic budget motel, well... good luck standing out in a sea of more visually appealing listings.

So how do you make your rental the kind of place people want to post about and, more importantly, **book**? Here's your playbook for making your property truly Instagrammable:

## How to Make Your Property More Instagrammable:

- **Add Statement Decor** – Think bold wallpaper, neon signs with cheeky phrases, or artistic furniture. A "But First, Coffee" neon sign near the kitchen? Instant photo op. An oversized rattan chair with plush cushions? That's a "cozy nook" post waiting to happen.

- **Create Photo-Worthy Spaces** – Guests love a **rooftop patio with fairy lights**, a **hanging egg chair with a view**, or even a **bathroom with a giant, freestanding tub and spa-like ambiance**. Give them spaces they can't resist snapping pics of!

- **Encourage Guest Photos** – Offer a small discount for guests who share their stay on Instagram and tag you. Bonus points if you create a unique hashtag for your rental (e.g., **#BeachBungalowViews** or **#CabinGoals**) to build organic social proof.

- **Use Unique & Cozy Lighting** – Harsh overhead lighting kills the vibe. Opt for **warm, dimmable lights**, bedside lamps, and **strategically placed LED strips** to create a soft, inviting atmosphere that looks *chef's kiss* on camera.

- **Lean into Themes** – A standard rental blends in, but a **boho jungle loft** or a **mid-century modern treehouse**? That stands out. Guests love a **strong aesthetic** that makes their stay feel like an experience.

- **Invest in a Killer View (If Possible)** – Got a rental near the mountains, the ocean, or a city skyline? **Make it the star of the show**. A well-placed hammock, a window seat, or even a simple bistro table on the balcony can turn an average space into a "must-book" spot.

- **Offer Instagrammable Amenities** – A swinging chair, an **outdoor projector setup**, a vintage record player—guests **love** unique features that elevate their experience *and* their feed.

## Why This Matters

The modern traveler isn't just looking for a place to stay—they're looking for an experience that fits their **personal aesthetic** and is worth sharing. The more "share-worthy" your property is, the **more organic exposure it gets**, which means more people seeing it, loving it, and ultimately **booking it**. In other words: make your place photogenic, and guests will do the marketing for you.

And let's not forget: **social media is the new word of mouth.** A guest tagging your rental and raving about their stay is the **modern version of a glowing referral**. So if you're not making your space Instagrammable, you're leaving bookings (and free marketing) on the table.

At the end of the day, people don't just want to book a stay. They want to book **a vibe, an aesthetic, a feeling**. Give them that, and they'll not only come—they'll bring their entire online audience with them. Now, who's ready to go buy a neon sign?

## Final Thoughts: What's Next for Short-Term Rentals?

The future of short-term rentals is **exciting, fast-paced, and full of opportunities**. The industry is shifting, and **staying ahead means embracing change before it happens**. Hosts who recognize these trends—whether it's through **sustainability, technology, or guest experience upgrades**—will be the ones who **turn challenges into opportunities and setbacks into growth.**

The best part? The possibilities are **endless**. Want to make your rental a sustainability haven? Guests are ready for it. Thinking of adding **tech-driven convenience**? People are already expecting it. Considering offering **curated experiences** to set your property apart? That's exactly where the industry is headed. The most successful hosts aren't just **reacting** to trends; they're **leading the way.**

Success isn't just about having a great property anymore. It's about **creating unforgettable experiences, adapting to new demands, and thinking beyond just a listing.** It's about building something bigger—**a brand, a reputation, and a thriving business that can weather any market shift**.

So stay curious, keep innovating, and remember—**the best hosts aren't just keeping up with trends, they're setting them.** Your future in short-term rentals isn't just promising—it's limitless.

# Chapter Twelve

# STR Success: Double-Check & Dominate!

**Common Pitfalls in STR Investments (And How to Dodge Them Like a Pro!)**

**STR Success Checklist: Use this quick checklist for you to refer to easily in order to dodge the most common short-term rental mistakes and set yourself up for STR success!**

**Market Research & Planning**

✔ Did you analyze the **demand in your area** using tools like AirDNA or Mashvisor?

✔ Have you checked **local STR regulations and permit requirements**?

✔ Are there **strong tourism, business, or event attractions** that will keep your STR booked?

✔ Have you researched **competitor pricing and amenities** to position your listing competitively?

## Financial Preparedness

✔ Do you have a **realistic budget** including mortgage, utilities, cleaning, supplies, and maintenance?

✔ Have you factored in **seasonal fluctuations** in occupancy?

✔ Do you have a **reserve fund** for unexpected expenses like repairs?

✔ Are you using **dynamic pricing tools** like PriceLabs, Wheelhouse, or Beyond Pricing?

## Property Setup & Design

✔ Did you furnish with **quality, comfortable furniture**, including a **great mattress**?

✔ Have you invested in **eye-catching decor** to make your STR stand out?

✔ Is the space **clutter-free and guest-ready**? (No personal items lying around!)

✔ Have you **optimized your listing photos** with professional-quality images?

✔ Is your home **functional** with essentials like extra towels, a coffee station, and toiletries?

## Guest Experience & Communication

✔ Do you send a **friendly welcome message** with check-in details?

✔ Have you provided a **house manual or digital guidebook** with Wi-Fi info, house rules, and local tips?

✔ Are you **responsive** to guest inquiries and issues within an hour?

✔ Do you offer **small extras** like a welcome basket or handwritten note?

✔ Have you made check-in/check-out **seamless and stress-free**?

## Maintenance & Operations

✔ Have you **hired a reliable cleaner** or set up a cleaning schedule?

✔ Is your property **stocked with essentials** (toilet paper, soap, kitchen basics)?

✔ Do you regularly check for **wear and tear** (broken appliances, leaky faucets, missing items)?

✔ Is your **Wi-Fi strong and reliable**? (Test it and advertise the speed in your listing!)

✔ Have you set up a **backup plan** for emergency maintenance?

## Long-Term Success & Growth

✔ Are you keeping up with **guest reviews** and making improvements based on feedback?

✔ Have you experimented with **promotions or discounts** to increase occupancy during slow periods?

✔ Do you update your **listing photos and descriptions regularly** to stay fresh in search rankings?

✔ Are you collecting **direct bookings** through your own website or social media?

✔ Have you built a **great reputation** that keeps guests coming back?

## Final Thought: STR Success is in the Details!

✔ If you checked **at least 90%** of these boxes—congrats! You're on your way to running a **top-tier STR**.

✔ If you **missed a few**, no worries—use this as your roadmap to **fine-tune your hosting strategy**!

This checklist keeps **your STR on track for success** and helps ensure **great guest experiences, repeat bookings, and long-term profitability**. Print it, save it, or revisit it whenever you need a **quick hosting refresh!**

Remember you started this journey with an idea—a spark of curiosity about what lies *beyond* Airbnb. Maybe you wanted to take back control, escape the uncertainty of ever-changing algorithms, or build something that wasn't dependent on a single platform. Whatever brought you here, you now have the knowledge, strategies, and confidence to create a thriving short-term rental business *on your terms.* No more waiting. No more relying on someone else's rules. You are in the driver's seat.

## The Power of Ownership

One of the most exciting things about stepping beyond Airbnb is the power of ownership. When you build a direct booking strategy, diversify across platforms, and expand your portfolio with intention, you create a business that truly belongs to *you*. It's not just about securing bookings—it's about building *a brand*. It's about knowing that if one platform changes its policies overnight, your business won't crumble. It's about creating long-term stability and real wealth that supports your vision and lifestyle.

And let's be honest—there's something incredibly rewarding about cutting out the middleman. Those 15-20% platform fees? You're putting them back in your pocket. The ability to communicate directly with guests, build relationships, and deliver personalized experiences? That's how you turn one-time visitors into *raving fans* who come back again and again.

## Success is Built on Action

The truth is, success in this business isn't reserved for the lucky few who stumble into the perfect property or hit the jackpot with an ideal market. The most successful short-term rental entrepreneurs are the ones who *take action.* They don't just sit around waiting for bookings to roll in—they market, they optimize, they test new strategies. They don't get stuck in fear of the unknown—they learn, adapt, and keep moving forward.

And that's exactly what I want for you. Maybe you're about to launch your first direct booking website. Maybe you're considering your next investment, exploring new platforms, or automating parts of your business to free up more of your time. No matter where you are, I challenge you to take that next step *now*. Because the difference between those who succeed and those who don't? It's not talent, luck, or resources—it's *action*.

## The Bigger Picture

Of course, this journey is about more than just bookings, profits, and expansion. It's about designing a *life* that works for you. Whether your goal is financial freedom, more time with family, the ability to travel, or simply the peace of mind that comes with being in control of your income, this business is a vehicle to help you get there.

And the best part? You get to decide what success looks like. Maybe that means owning a few well-run properties that generate passive income while you focus on other passions. Maybe it means scaling into a full-fledged empire with multiple properties in different locations. Whatever your vision is, know that it's *possible.* You're not just a host. You're an entrepreneur, a creator, and a leader in this industry.

## Chapter Thirteen

# When to Sell, Upgrade, or Expand to Build a Powerful Property Portfolio

Building a profitable short-term rental business isn't just about hosting guests—it's about making **strategic, high-impact money moves** that ensure long-term success. The difference between a casual host and a true short-term rental mogul comes down to **knowing when to sell, when to upgrade, and when to expand.** Think of it like chess: Are you **clinging to a pawn** when you could be making a game-changing move and securing your queen? Every property in your portfolio should be **working just as hard as you do**—bringing in consistent income, growing in value, and helping you achieve financial freedom.

The short-term rental market is constantly evolving, and as an investor, your ability to **adapt, optimize, and scale** will determine your success. Some properties serve their purpose but eventually reach their peak performance, signaling that it's time to **cash out and reinvest elsewhere.** Others have untapped potential that, with the right upgrades, could **dramatically increase your profits.** And then there's expansion—the ultimate power move that allows you to **diversify, increase revenue streams, and future-proof your business.**

This chapter will guide you through the **key signs and financial indicators** that tell you whether it's time to sell, upgrade, or expand. You'll learn how to analyze market trends, assess property performance, and make **data-driven decisions** that maximize your returns. Whether you're aiming to fine-tune your current investments or take your portfolio to the next level, understanding these strategies will ensure that **every property in your line up is a high-performing asset, not just another piece on the board.**

## When to Sell: Time to Cash Out?

Sometimes, the best move is to say **"Thank you, next"** to a property. How do you know it's time to **let go and cash in**? Here's when selling makes sense:

- **Your property has appreciated like crazy** – If your place has significantly increased in value and you're sitting on a mountain of equity, selling could allow you to **cash out while the market is in your favor.** The key here is to analyze comparable sales in your area and assess whether reinvesting in a higher-yielding option makes sense. If selling today could fund the purchase of two properties tomorrow, **that's a wealth-building move worth considering.**

- **Bookings are dropping and not bouncing back** – Maybe your rental was once the darling of the market, but now it's **struggling to stay booked.** Oversaturation, regulatory changes, or shifting travel patterns can all impact occupancy rates. If you find yourself slashing prices just to get guests through the door—or worse, struggling to get bookings at all—it might be time to pivot. **Selling before your asset depreciates further can protect your profits and allow you to reinvest in a stronger market.**

- **Maintenance costs are bleeding you dry** – Some properties just don't age gracefully. If your STR has become a bottomless money pit with endless repairs, major structural issues, or high upkeep costs, it may be time to **stop pouring money into a sinking ship.** The moment maintenance expenses start outpacing profits is the moment to seriously consider selling. A property that requires constant attention **not only drains your cash flow but also your energy and time.** Let it go and put that capital into a rental that requires less effort and delivers more returns.

- **A bigger and better opportunity is calling** – In the world of STR investing, **opportunity knocks loudly.** Maybe a multi-unit property with significantly higher revenue potential has come onto your radar. Perhaps a luxury rental in a prime vacation destination is within reach. When an opportunity arises that could **exponentially grow your earnings**, selling an underperforming or stagnant asset to **fund a better investment is a smart move.**

Think of it this way: If your current property is delivering decent but not outstanding returns, and you have the chance to step into a **higher-yielding investment**, the smart investor sells, reinvests, and keeps growing. **Your goal is to move toward assets that make your money work harder for you.**

Before you throw in the towel on a property, ask yourself: **Can a few tweaks turn this place into a gold mine?** A little **STR Botox** (aka renovations) might be all you need to boost occupancy and profits. Think of it as a glow-up for your rental—because let's be real, nobody wants to stay in a place that looks like it hasn't been touched since flip phones were cutting-edge technology.

- **Your décor is still living in 2010** – If your rental looks more like a time capsule than an Insta-worthy retreat, it's time for a refresh. Modern furniture, bold color accents, and stylish details can **increase perceived value overnight**. Your guests want a space they can brag about on social media, not one that reminds them of their grandma's basement.

- **You're missing key amenities that guests love** – No smart lock? No high-speed Wi-Fi? No coffee station? **Big mistake.** Today's guests expect convenience, and small upgrades can **justify a higher nightly rate and keep guests coming back.** A good rule of thumb: If a guest has ever messaged you with "Do you have a...?" and the answer was "No," consider adding it!

- **The competition is crushing you** – If neighboring properties are **offering more for the same price**, you need to step up your game. Whether it's adding a **hot tub, upgrading the outdoor space, or investing in a killer mattress**, the little things can set you apart. Pro tip: Check out your competitors' listings and steal (ethically, of course) their best ideas.

- **Your target guest profile has changed** – Maybe your rental was set up for budget travelers, but you realize **luxury couples' getaways are where the real money is**. If your current setup screams "backpackers on a budget," but your area is trending toward high-end stays, consider a rebrand. Swapping bunk beds for a king-size with plush bedding might be the difference between a $50-a-night stay and a $200-a-night experience.

A few well-placed upgrades can turn a struggling rental into a **high-demand, high-revenue powerhouse**. Remember, in the STR game, perception is everything. The goal is to make guests feel like they're getting a **premium experience—even if you didn't spend a premium to provide it.**

## When to Expand: Go Big or Go Home?

You've mastered your current rental(s), and now you're **itching to grow**. But when is the right time to expand? Here's how to know **you're ready to scale**:

- **Your current STR is maxed out** – If you've optimized pricing, nailed your occupancy rates, and leveraged direct bookings, **congrats, you're ready for the next move!** If you're consistently booked and can't increase your rates much more, adding another property could be the natural next step.

- **Market conditions are screaming "BUY NOW"** – If interest rates are low, property values are stable, and demand for short-term rentals is growing, it might be time to **snatch up a new investment while the conditions are right.** Keep an eye on trends in travel, local tourism, and real estate market cycles.

- **You can expand without risking financial ruin** – Growth is great, but not at the cost of your peace of mind. Make sure you have the funds (or creative financing options like partnerships, joint ventures, or seller financing) to expand **without drowning in debt**. Smart investors scale sustainably, not recklessly.

- **You're diversifying your locations** – Relying on one market is risky. Expanding into a different city, state, or even a seasonal location can **balance your revenue year-round**. A property in a ski town can complement one in a beach destination, ensuring steady income no matter the season.

- **You have systems in place to manage growth** – If managing one property has you pulling your hair out, adding more might be a disaster. Before expanding, ensure you have **automation, a reliable team, and streamlined operations** in place. Hiring a co-host, implementing property management software, or outsourcing guest communication can make scaling much smoother.

Expanding is about **working smarter, not harder**. If you're hitting all these marks, it's probably time to go big

## Final Thoughts: The Smart Way to Scale

**Evaluate Your Current Portfolio** – Take a hard look at your short-term rental(s). Are they performing at peak potential? Are they generating the kind of returns you expected? If not, identify the problem areas and determine whether a sale, an upgrade, or better marketing could improve performance.

**Run the Numbers** – Never make a decision based on gut feelings alone. Crunch the data to see if selling, upgrading, or expanding makes financial sense. Are you sitting on untapped equity that could be reinvested for higher returns? Could a simple renovation significantly boost your revenue? Numbers never lie—let them guide you.

**Study Market Trends** – Timing is everything. Pay attention to **interest rates, local STR regulations, tourism trends, and competitor pricing.** A booming market could be the perfect opportunity to expand, while an oversaturated one might signal that it's time to pivot or cash out. Always stay ahead of industry shifts.

**Leverage Direct Bookings** – If you haven't already, start optimizing your **direct booking strategy.** Reducing reliance on third-party platforms like Airbnb and Vrbo means **higher profits and more control** over your business. This added stability can make expansion easier and more predictable.

**Create a Scalable System** – Growth is only sustainable if you have **systems in place**. Streamline your operations with automation, hire reliable cleaners and co-hosts, and use **property management software** to handle guest communication, pricing adjustments, and maintenance requests. The more hands-off your current STRs are, the easier it will be to scale.

**Develop a Clear Vision for Expansion** – Where do you want to be in 5 years? Do you want to dominate a specific market, diversify across different locations, or build a mix of luxury and budget-friendly rentals? Define your growth plan now so that each investment you make aligns with your ultimate goals.

**Surround Yourself with Experts** – Whether it's networking with other STR owners, consulting real estate agents, or hiring a mentor, learning from those who've already mastered the game will **accelerate your success.** Stay educated, adapt, and never stop refining your approach.

## Your Next Move Could Unlock Your Biggest Financial Win Yet

The STR industry is dynamic, and those who **think ahead, act decisively, and adapt quickly** are the ones who thrive. Whether you're selling for profit, upgrading for better returns, or expanding your empire, every move should align with your **bigger picture**.

# Chapter Fourteen

# Conclusion

Congratulations! You've made it to the end of *Short Stays, Big Pay*—but in reality, this is just the beginning of your short-term rental (STR) journey. If you've made it this far, you've armed yourself with the knowledge, strategies, and tools needed to build a highly profitable short-term rental business. But remember, knowledge without action is just potential. It's what you do with this information that will determine your success.

Throughout this book, we've covered everything you need to **transform short stays into big paydays** and secure your financial future through STRs. Let's take a moment to reflect on what we've accomplished together:

- **Finding the Right Property** – You now know how to evaluate markets, analyze potential properties, and calculate ROI to make informed investment decisions.

- **Setting Up for Success** – From interior design and amenities to creating a welcoming guest experience, we've covered what it takes to stand out in a competitive market.
- **Listing Optimization & Pricing Strategies** – You've learned how to craft a high-converting listing, use professional photography, write compelling descriptions, and set smart, dynamic pricing to maximize revenue.
- **The Power of Direct Bookings** – We dove into how to break free from high platform fees, build a strong brand, and leverage marketing to attract guests directly, putting **more money in your pocket**.
- **Mastering Hospitality & Guest Experience** – You now understand how to wow your guests with five-star service, handle issues with grace, and turn one-time visitors into loyal, repeat customers.
- **Scaling & Expanding Your Portfolio** – We explored the right time to reinvest, creative financing options, and strategies to multiply your success while minimizing risk.
- **Automation & Efficiency Hacks** – By leveraging smart tools, self-check-in options, and streamlined operations, you can run your STR empire with **less effort and more profit**.

At this point, you might be feeling excited, overwhelmed, or even a little nervous—and that's completely normal. But here's the thing: **you don't need to have it all figured out to get started.** The most successful hosts weren't experts when they launched their first listing. They learned, adapted, and improved over time.

The key now is **taking action.** Start with what you have, where you are. Whether you're analyzing your first deal, updating an existing listing, or working on your direct booking strategy, every step forward is a step closer to financial freedom.

## Your Next Steps

1. **Take Immediate Action** – Revisit the chapters that resonated most with you and create a game plan. Maybe it's setting up your first listing, optimizing pricing, or launching your direct booking website. Whatever it is, commit to doing it **now.**

2. **Stay Curious & Keep Learning** – The STR industry evolves, and staying ahead means continuously learning. Follow trends, listen to successful hosts, and adapt your strategies as needed.

3. **Join a Community of Like-Minded Hosts** – Surround yourself with people who understand the STR business. Engage in forums, attend meetups, or join mastermind groups to stay motivated and inspired.

4. **Track Your Progress & Scale Smartly** – Set clear goals, measure performance, and don't be afraid to reinvest in growing

your business. The sooner you scale, the sooner you'll unlock the full potential of STR wealth.

5. **Celebrate Your Wins** – Whether it's your first direct booking, a glowing five-star review, or hitting your revenue goal, take the time to celebrate your successes. These milestones are proof that you're on the right path.

## Final Thoughts

Short-term rentals are more than just an income stream—they're a **gateway to financial independence, freedom, and a lifestyle on your terms.** Whether you're looking to quit your 9-to-5, build generational wealth, or simply enjoy an extra source of income, the opportunity is **right in front of you.**

So what are you waiting for? **It's time to take that first step.** You have the blueprint. You have the strategies. Now, it's up to you to put them into action.

And remember—this isn't goodbye, it's just the beginning. I'd love to hear about your journey! Connect with me, share your wins, and let's continue building your success together.

Here's to **short stays, big pay, and an even bigger future ahead**

# About the author

**Michelle Ward – The Queen of Short-Term Rentals (and Master of Doing Things Her Own Way)**

Michelle isn't just another STR host—**she's a powerhouse in the world of short-term rentals**, a direct booking enthusiast, and a business strategist who knows exactly how to turn properties into **cash-generating guest magnets**.

Before stepping into the world of hospitality, Michelle spent years in **management for major online media and publishing companies**, leading teams, managing staff, and navigating the fast-paced digital world. But after countless meetings, overflowing inboxes, and way too many corporate jargon-filled emails, she decided it was time to **trade deadlines for direct bookings and carve out a life on her own terms**.

What started as a side hustle quickly became a **six-figure rental empire**, proving that smart strategies, a knack for branding, and just the right amount of charm can turn short-term rentals into a **seriously profitable business**. Now, Rae's portfolio is thriving, her guest ratings are sky-high, and she's mastered the art of creating **memorable stays that keep guests coming back for more**.

Her philosophy? **Hosting is both an experience and a business.** A sparkling clean home, a personal touch, and a strategic approach to marketing will always beat **algorithm-chasing and hoping for the best.** She's all about **taking control, diversifying income streams, and showing other hosts how to escape the grip of high-fee platforms and build a truly independent rental business.**

When Michelle isn't busy **outsmarting Airbnb's algorithm** or crafting the perfect guest experience, you'll find her **sipping coffee at a reasonable hour (because there's no more 6 AM commutes), traveling the world, and enjoying the flexibility she built for herself.** Whether it's **mentoring other hosts, fine-tuning her properties, or making the most of her location-independent lifestyle**, she's living proof that **a well-run short-term rental business isn't just about making money—it's about creating freedom**.

And if you ever catch her binge-watching a series in the middle of the day? **That's not procrastination—that's a well-earned reward for taking control of her business and making it work for her.**

## Want to Learn More? Check Out My Other Book!

## Take Your STR Business to the Next Level!

If you're serious about elevating your short-term rental business, don't stop here! My other books go even deeper into **advanced hosting strategies, direct booking mastery, and financial growth beyond Airbnb.**

**Airbnb Mastery** – Ready to move beyond the basics? This is the ultimate guide for experienced hosts looking to **optimize, scale, and maximize profits**. Learn how to streamline operations, master dynamic pricing, and automate guest communication, so your business runs efficiently—even when you're not involved.

Discover the power of **direct bookings** and multiple revenue streams, ensuring long-term success beyond Airbnb's platform. If you're ready to expand your portfolio, boost efficiency, and transform your rental into a true passive income stream, this book is your roadmap to financial freedom.

Don't just manage an STR—**build a thriving, scalable business** that generates wealth and works for you!

For full list of my books, go to: michellewardbooks.com

# References & Suggested Reading

### 1. Short-Term Rental Industry Reports & Market Trends

- Airbnb Official Reports
- STR (Smith Travel Research) Reports
- AirDNA Market Data
- Skift Short-Term Rental Industry Trends

### 2. Direct Booking Strategies & Revenue Management

- Mark Simpson, *The Book Direct Playbook* (Boostly)
- Heather Bayer, *Vacation Rental Success* Podcast & Blog
- Rent Responsibly (Advocacy & Education)
- PriceLabs (Dynamic Pricing Tool)

## 3. Legal & Regulatory Considerations

- Short-Term Rental Laws by City
- American Hotel & Lodging Association (AHLA) Reports
- STR Insurance Guide (Proper Insurance)

## 4. Hospitality & Guest Experience Best Practices

- *The Airbnb Story* by Leigh Gallagher
- *The Art of Hospitality* by Micah Solomon
- The Superhost Academy (Airbnb's training & resources)
- The Boutique Hotel Playbook by Daniel Rusteen

## 5. Digital Marketing & SEO for STRs

- Neil Patel's Digital Marketing Blog
- Moz SEO Guide for Vacation Rentals
- HubSpot Content Marketing for Hospitality

## 6. Financial Planning & Wealth Building from STRs

- *Rich Dad Poor Dad* by Robert Kiyosaki (for wealth mindset)
- *The Millionaire Real Estate Investor* by Gary Keller
- BiggerPockets Real Estate Investing Podcasts

Made in the USA
Monee, IL
04 November 2026

67380870R00118